Right Decisions

Walking In Wisdom

J.H. Marzola

Copyright © 2014 James Marzola

All rights reserved.

ISBN-10: 069220590X
ISBN-13: 978-0692205907

Dedication

This book is dedicated my parents, Orlando and Dee Marzola. Early in my life, they taught me to think.

Thank you, Dad, for always giving us not just the words, but the example of what is right in a man.

Thank you, Mom, for being love demonstrated.

Here are some words of wisdom I remember most growing up:

- *You can only do what you can do.*
- *Always pay the few dollars more for quality because you'll long forget how much you paid in the first place.*
- *If you don't have the time to do it right the first time, when will you find the time to do it right the second time?*
- *If you want to get something done, give it to a busy person.*
- *Always know what down it is and the location of the first down marker.*
- *Two wrongs don't make a right.*

- *If your mom is happy, I'm happy.*
- *Where's the paddle?*

A Special Thanks

I also want to thank my wonderful wife, Loretta, for her enduring patience and constant encouragement to help move me along the way to complete this book. I love you.

Children are God's gift, and each one is precious in His sight. Nadine, Riley, Adam, Gordon, Stephen, and Jordan: please keep wisdom in mind as you find your way and recognize God's plan for your life. Be useful and look for ways to help others. You may not be able to change the world, but you can change one person's world.

Finally, I want to thank Alexandra, my editor who reviewed the book for me and gave valuable insight, especially with my punctuation.

Table of Contents

Dedication iii

A Special Thanks iv

Introduction vii

Day One – Beginning of Knowledge 9

Day Two – The Value of Wisdom 16

Day Three – Rewards of Wisdom 20

Day Four – Instruction 24

Day Five – Pitfalls of Immorality 27

Day Six – The Perils 30

Day Seven – Choices 37

Day Eight – Wisdom and Folly 40

Day Nine – Contrasts Part I 43

Day Ten – Contrasts Part II 46

Day Eleven – Contrasts Part III 52

Day Twelve – Attitude 57

Day Thirteen – Listening 63

Day Fourteen – Belief 70

Day Fifteen – The Words You Use 79

Day Sixteen – Our Activity 85

Day Seventeen - Justice 92

Day Eighteen - Trust 97

Day Nineteen - Integrity 102

Day Twenty – Be Prepared 107

Day Twenty-One – Conduct Part I 112

Day Twenty-Two – Conduct Part II 117

Day Twenty Three - Evaluation 121

Day Twenty-Four – The People You Meet 125

Day Twenty-Five – Relationships Part I 130

Day Twenty-Six – Relationships Part II 136

Day Twenty-Seven – Actions We Take Part I ... 141

Day Twenty-Eight – Actions We Take Part II ... 147

Day Twenty-Nine – Actions We Take Part III ... 151

Day Thirty – Words to Live By 158

Day Thirty-One – Who You Want to Be 162

Introduction

The inspiration and encouragement for writing this book came from reading the Book of Proverbs each and every day for the past several years. The more I read Proverbs, the more convinced I became that wisdom is a limited and precious commodity in our society.

So what is wisdom anyway? Simply put, wisdom is knowing what to do and when to do it. Wisdom is not about the intelligence you were born with, but rather about common sense.

Why should you care? Wisdom, the putting into practice common sense, helps protect you from making the mistakes that are avoidable.

What you are about to read is not a verse by verse commentary. I take God's admonishment in Proverbs 30:6 seriously: *"Do not add to His words lest He reprove you, and you be proved a liar."* My goal was to take what God gave us in the Book of Proverbs and "translate" it, from my perspective, into today's language as a reflection of the circumstances of our modern lives. It is my attempt to share what I learned from Proverbs and perhaps give you a reason to read Proverbs for yourself.

This book has 31 chapters, as does the Book of Proverbs. My advice is to read one chapter each day of the month, and then do it again. While you are at it...try reading the rest of the books of the Bible. You may find a new appreciation of God's love.

One final note. The book is written from a man's point of view. The principle's work for women and men.

Day One
The Beginning of Knowledge

The beginning is always the most important because how you begin something tends to set the course of your direction as well as the habits you create. Stephen Covey's book, *"The Seven Habits,"* says that *"the carpenter measures twice and cuts once,"* because if you start off even slightly wrong, you end up very wrong when you finish.

The beginning of this journey starts with embracing wisdom and instruction. It is not just a feeling nor an assent of the mind. It is a pursuit. It is a passion.

The goal is to know wisdom and instruction, and to understand words of insight. It is about receiving instruction on how to operate wisely so that you are dealing in ways that are right, just, honest, and fair to others. This right beginning is also about giving back to others. It means to give insight to those who may not understand as you do and to give those who are young guidance and ideas on how to be careful in their decision process.

So what is wisdom? Some say wisdom is the

working out of knowledge in practical ways. A person may know something, but practicing it is completely different. It means to comprehend the consequences of one's actions. Wisdom is the ability to "see" far enough down the road to discern which path to take or maybe not take at all.

As you begin your daily process, remember to start your day with a prayer. It opens your mind and heart to understand what wisdom is, to know the words of the wise, and to realize that what you have is a gift from God. Wisdom, knowledge and understanding all come from the Lord.

Those who choose to disregard this really despise wisdom and instruction; they put themselves in a mindset of not being teachable or coachable. You know this person. You work with them. They have a short attention span and they seem to cut you off when you talk. They do not pay attention to what you say, and they want to tell you what they know.

This attitude reminds me of some of the behaviors of my children when they were young, especially entering their teenage years. I had a conversation with each of them to let them know that they were entering into one of the most special times of their lives. No one can explain it and they should take full advantage of it because it only lasts a few years. I told them that it ended when they turned 20. I explained to them that turning 13, they enter this strange dimension where they will *"know everything."* No matter what I said, what their mother said, what their teachers or coaches said they would already know it. You may recall the phrase; maybe you used it, too. No matter what was said, the response was, *"I know."*

When someone has an attitude, a conviction that they *"know it,"* there is little they can learn. Legendary coach John Wooden says it this way: *"It's what you learn after you know everything that really matters."*

Watch Out

With every good beginning, there are obstacles and distractions that will limit your progress or might even keep you from your destination.

Focus on what you want to accomplish and keep it in front of you. If you keep (protect) what you learned, the reason why you are doing what you are doing, it becomes a reminder to you. It is similar to wearing a hat on your head that protects you from the elements; you forget it is there until you need it.

Many times we read or hear the word "if." Many times it is in the context of, *"if someone entices you..."* My opinion is that more times than not, this little word "if" is really the word "since." I say that because 100% of the time we are enticed (tempted) to get distracted from our goal or objective as we begin our journey. It is not an "if," it is a certainty "since."

Therefore, since you will be enticed, be ready for it. Expect it. How do you expect it? You have to look past who is enticing you to what they are enticing you to do. The reason I say this is because many times the "who" that entices us may be those close to us: our friends, family members, spouse, parents, and business associates. It is not that they mean us harm. Usually it is just the opposite. They think they know what is best for us and want to protect us from the consequences of making a bad decision. Other times it will be from left field, out of the blue, and quite tempting. These are the ones you really need to inspect by understanding what they want you to be involved with and why.

So evaluate what they want from you and why they want it, and determine if it is a distraction or an enhancement to your journey. Ask the following questions.

- *Is it something they want you to keep secret? In other words, do they want you*

> *to not tell anyone else or get outside advice?*
> - *Is it something that will take advantage of others so you can profit from it?*
> - *Is this a "partnership" where everyone will share in the profits together?*
> - *Are they looking to use your good name and reputation to legitimize the action that they want to take?*
> - *Does this look like something that excites the "getting something for nothing" side in all of us?*

If you answered "yes" to any of these questions, be careful and turn away from this enticement. Once you say yes, you enter a path where the results are not what you expected, and you will, like a bird trapped in a net, be unable to get yourself free.

Instruction is all around you

We live in a society that gives us access to all sorts of instruction. We have libraries, books on CD, e-books, blogs, networking sites, internet-based learning programs; you can learn when and how you want to learn it.

What if you exchanged 15 minutes each day of listening to the radio, talking on the phone, watching TV, surfing the net or updating Facebook for learning something new? Even if you do this just five days a week, you will invest 65 hours a year to improving yourself.

I made this statement many times when interviewing candidates for various job openings over the last 30 years. It did not matter if they were in sales, marketing, technical consulting, software development, accounting, or law. *"There's a big difference with someone having ten years of true experience and a person with one year of experience that they repeated for ten years."* What kind of person will you be ten years from now?

Life is what you make it. If you invest the time, if you seek wisdom and instruction, you prepare yourself for what life brings your way. If you refuse, time eventually brings about events and you are compelled to say "I wish I had..." instead of, "I'm glad I did."

Begin your journey today by seeking God's wisdom for your life.

"How long will you love being simple, naive in your thinking and in your actions? Fools hate knowledge and instruction." Proverbs 1:22

Take an inventory of your thoughts, actions, and attitudes when it comes to your path and the practices you perform each day.

If not, *"You will eat the fruit of your choices, you will drink the bitter cup of your making."* *Proverbs 1:31*

But whoever listens to what God has prescribed in Walking in Wisdom, will be secure, sure, and without dread of disaster.

Day Two
The Value of Wisdom

What do you value? Each of us places different values on different things. You have heard it said that we really do not know the true value of something until we no longer have it.

What if you were too dull in your senses to not know what you do not know; that you are actually missing something and you do not even know it?

How would you like the opposite; to have protection, the right information, be kept from bad choices, be prevented from poor decisions, and from unscrupulous people, and not even know that this is happening to you?

This is the basis of Day Two in your journey. However, like anything of value, if you want it and appreciate it, you must expend effort towards it.

So what effort do you need to expend? It is the energy of the will, of the mind, of your heart, of your choices. God always starts with the heart. He starts with the inside because if the inside is not right, then for certain the outside (what we do) does not matter.

Do you treasure what God treasures? Are you receptive to what God says about right and wrong? Effort is necessary today and every day to focus on what is wise, to direct your heart to the understanding of the people in your life and what is going on around you.

Remember the feeling when your heart ached or when your voice cried out for that something that you thought you would die without it? If you will cry for discernment, the ability to make good choices when you do not have all the facts, and lift up your voice for understanding, if you will seek wisdom as though it was precious, like gold or silver, or search for it as though it was the Lost Dutchman's mine, then and only then, will you understand the value of what Walking in Wisdom brings to you.

What is that value? Here is my take away:

- *Discern the reverence of the LORD.*
- *Discover the knowledge of God.*
- *Differentiate what is right and just and every good course of action that needs taking.*
- *Discretion (foresight, carefulness) will guard your decisions.*
- *Understanding of situations will watch over you.*

All of these lead to the same place:

1. To deliver you from the way of evil. In other words, keeps you from doing something that is going to cause you or others harm.

2. Protect you from those who speak words to persuade you to do things that are off the path *you should follow.*

3. Protect you from those whose life's course of actions are to do what is wrong or those who are willing to live their life in a way that is on the edge of being wrong.

Men seem to be more easily tempted to stray from home, from their wife, and the covenant to be faithful and true.

Walking in Wisdom helps deliver us from one of the most seductive approaches by another woman: *flattery*.

All men have egos; some of us are lead away by flattery because we care what others say about us and that makes us vulnerable.

You may be thinking that you do not have such a big ego and feel protected. Your ego is bigger than you think. When you feel unappreciated and have a *"woe is me, I do all the work, no one understands how hard I work"* feeling, your ego is running at full speed. Add to this mixture the right environment at work or the right social setting.

Maybe you travel out of town too. Insert the the right amount of flattery by an encouraging woman, and the thoughts and temptation to stray begin.

Nothing good comes from straying from the path of fidelity.

Where will you end up?
Walking in Wisdom leads you to a path of quality choices and will keep you on the path to do what is right.

Those who live an honest life comprehend and understand the blessings they have. The opposite is also true. Those who live their lives in a way that defines their character as immoral or disingenuous, do not comprehend the blessings they have.

Day Three
The Rewards of Wisdom

All throughout our journey we are prone to distractions. This is why we are encouraged *"not to forget"* what we learn along the way. What we commit to our heart is what we keep close to us. Keep these principles of wisdom close to your heart.

Kindness and truth are two characteristics that are always in high demand.

People may not like when you speak the truth or say what is right, but they will respect you for it. This is a trait that others admire even if they do not directly tell you.

Everyone craves a disciplined life. Speaking the truth and acting in kindness are two disciplines that make a big difference.

We have a tendency to be kind to the people we respect or those in a place of authority over us. We act quite differently toward those we do not know or those closest to us. Sharp tones and brutal comments tend to come easier. We can make a secretary or a clerk feel disrespected and degraded just because we do not see them as being important to us.

Kindness is something deep inside that works its way to the surface to treat everyone with respect and appreciation. Acting this way will bring you favor from both God and man.

Faith

Trust is a temperamental fancy we have. We trust the chair we want to sit on believing it will hold up when we sit on it; we trust that the elevator will go to the floor we select.

We have a hard time trusting that if we lean on God's principles and not on what we think is the right direction, things will go well. If we take the time to acknowledge the way of God's wisdom, He will direct us onto the right path.

"Trust in the Lord with all your heart and lean not on your own understanding; in all your ways acknowledge Him and He will make your paths straight." Proverbs 3:5-6

It is easy for me to look to my past experiences, my past wins, my past failures, and allow those to guide my decisions because I believe in myself. Yet the best course of action is to look to God in reverence, He knows what is right for me and to turn me away from what is wrong. If I turn from what is evil and trust in what God's principles are, then peace will follow my decision making.

Course Correction

As a parent, we love our children and it is our responsibility to guide them into making right and wise decisions. We use various methods to correct them with the goal of getting their attention to help them examine their actions. It is important to use these times of correction as valuable teachable moments.

There are times in our life when we do not understand why something did not go the way we planned or expected. You may not realize why you were not given the promotion or the job offer. This is what I call a "course correction." Look at course corrections in your life as a blessing from God who loves you and is ultimately looking to bless you.

Silver and Gold

Ben Franklin once said *"empty the coins in your purse into your mind and your mind will fill your purse with coins."* Money comes and goes, but what makes the difference is understanding how to earn money regardless of circumstances.

There is peace in this pursuit as well as happiness. Wisdom is what God used to create the earth and all that is in it. Therefore, wisdom and understanding needs to be our pursuit as well.

Protection
The more I keep wisdom in my sight and close to me, like a necklace around my neck, the more secure my day-to-day life is. I sleep easier at night because I am not troubled about what I said or did.

Helpful
Wisdom also moves me to be compassionate and helpful. If I see someone in need and I have the means to help them, I need to act on that opportunity instead of coming up with some sort of reason to do something tomorrow to help that person. *"Do not withhold good from those to whom it is due, when it is in your power to do it." Proverbs 3:27*

I also need to be a good neighbor and not look for ways to take advantage of others. I must look for ways to help and not to fight with others just for the sake of gaining an advantage if that person has done me no harm. If they did harm you, then you have all the rights within the law and your conscience to right yourself.

The more I choose to do what is right in the ways of God, the closer a relationship I can have with Him. The more I look for ways to be devious and am foolish in my decision making, the more I move away from God and His blessings.

Day Four
A Father's Instruction

The true father has a heart filled with love and interest in providing what is best for his children. Walking in Wisdom is no different. That is why the writer of Proverbs is pleading with his listeners to give attention to his instructions so they will gain understanding.

He is passing on the instruction given to him by his father; he received instruction the same way, being told to *"let your heart hold fast my words; keep my commandments and live." Proverbs 4:4* His instruction is to acquire wisdom! Acquire understanding! Wisdom is like a woman that is not to be forsaken but one who you guard and protect. Love her and she will watch over you.

The beginning of wisdom is always the desire to acquire wisdom. If you prize her, wisdom will exalt you and honor you.

The father is reminding the child of his instruction, his direction in Walking in Wisdom that leads to the right path.

When you Walk
Walking is a metaphor of the way we conduct ourselves, the paths we chose to pursue in life,

the choices we make. If I embrace Walking in Wisdom, then the steps I take are not hindered. As I go faster in my journey, I will not stumble because wisdom is a normal part of my life.

The direction we take when we walk has choices.

It is my choice, no one else's, to enter onto the path of the wicked and go the way of evil men. What is your definition of wicked, evil men? Are the people you associate with looking for ways to take advantage of others? Do they look for ways to make people stumble or fall? If so, avoid them.

The contrast of this is those who walk in the path of what is right. Their path will shine brighter and brighter, just like the sun rising high in the sky after sunrise.

The more time you invest in Walking in Wisdom, the more you will notice the darkness.

The opposite is also true. Those who look to take advantage of people do not realize they are living in darkness. They will not recognize what they hinders them. They will blame others for their setbacks and problems.

What's Important
The father once again implores the child to keep his sayings and words of wisdom close to him, to keep them in his sight and keep them in his heart.

The results of this is life, health, and peace.

Watch over your heart with all diligence, for from it flow the springs of life." Proverbs 4:23
The implication here is that there are forces in this life that want to turn your heart away from what is right. You must be mindful of this and take steps to protect what is right. This is the life that can help others.

The father then instructs the child to do the following: *Proverbs 4:24-27*

- *Put away a deceitful mouth (lying and deception).*
- *Eliminate devious speech (talk and language that misleads).*
- *Look directly ahead with your eyes (focus on what is in front of you).*
- *Let your gaze be in front of you (look down the path and not to the sides of the road).*
- *Watch the path of your feet and your ways will be established (if you always take the right path, will you ever get lost?).*
- *Do not turn off the path to the right or left. You know what's right and what's wrong. Keep your feet from evil and your body will be kept away, too.*

Day Five
Pitfalls of Immorality

The writer of Proverbs is pleading as a father does to his children to give attention to his wisdom and to "incline one's ear" to listen to his understanding. The instruction is to observe discretion and reserve one's lips for knowledge; the contrast to this is, *"an adulteress' lips drip of honey and her speech is smoother than oil". Proverbs 5:3*

This is a metaphor for all that is going to distract you with its enticements as well as the lure of sexual temptations.

Temptation from the opposite sex usually begins with some kind of flattery - words that make you feel good about yourself. Distractions are also a temptation; they, too, are ones that look enticing and make you feel good. But what is the end result? You succumb to the sexual temptation and/or the other sensual distraction. The end of such deeds hurt like you were cut with a sharp knife. You feel like you want to die.

The best way to fight temptation(s) of all kinds is to flee from them. If you know you will drink with your friends at the bar, then do not go to the bar. If you do not want to gamble, do not go to the casino. We think it is much harder than it is. Avoid what you know will trip you up. And find someone you can call who can encourage you in your decision.

Keep far away from temptations and the places they lurk. If not, all your hard work will end up in ruin. How many times have we heard of the one indiscretion that destroyed a marriage, a family, a career? Or that one and only time someone tried a drug only to have it end their life.

I am sure you are saying to yourself that you are different, better, that this would never happen to you. Remember, pride comes before the fall. Avoid the temptation along with the people who lead you into temptation, and you spare your life from the turmoil it brings. If not, when the storm hits, you will say, *"how I hated instruction and did not listen to the voice of my teachers." Proverbs 5:12-13*

If you are married, remember the covenant that you made to be faithful to your spouse.

It is easy for men to succumb to sexual temptations. Women take heed as well.

A married man is to find pleasure in his wife, to *"drink water from his own well"* and *"rejoice in the wife of your youth." Proverbs 5:15 and 5:18*

Rejoice, what a vibrant, exciting word. Remember back to the early days of your dating, your engagement, and your wedding ceremony? Those are the anchor points on which to hold onto as temptations arise to lure you away from the covenant you made. Look to your wife or your husband to find sexual satisfaction and not in others be they real or a fantasy.

All is seen
We fail to realize that all that we do, God sees. He watches all the paths we take.

The sins we commit will hold us captive; keep us tied up.

Once we do something we never did before, it becomes easier each time to do it again. Before you know it, the habits you keep are the habits that keep you.

Remember the poem, *"sow a thought, reap an action; sow an action, reap a habit; sow a habit, reap a lifestyle; sow a lifestyle, reap a destiny."*

Day Six
The Perils of Debt

Today's instruction is for all of us who find ourselves in debt.

Walking in Wisdom talks about the necessity to get out of debt as quickly as possible. If you are in debt you are in bondage, a servant to the one you owe money to. All the work you do centers around how to pay for those obligations.

There are two kinds of debts to be aware of: those we make financially and those we make verbally.

Look at how many unnecessary financial debts we create and then feel trapped because of them, from a large mortgage to automobile and retail debt. Most of our debts happen because we make an emotional decision to buy and then justify it logically.

The habit of financing our purchases begins early in our adult lives. Most parents do not teach their children (especially through example) that unrestrained use of credit can be your enemy. Credit can be your friend, but most people do not know the principles of how to handle credit to their advantage. They become the willing victim of the lender. Usually there is no immediate consequence to the credit habit. If we feel no pain at the time of purchase, it is difficult to make the right decision.

Walking in Wisdom is different. It is an act of faith; it takes courage to curb desires and wants and look only to what you need. If you cannot pay cash for something or budget for it, then is it really needed? Notice I did not say is it "wanted"? We need very few things.

The other debt we find ourselves in is the debt of our verbal commitments. You want to be a person of integrity, of doing what you say you will do. Therefore, be careful to what you commit to, and then once you do, stick with it.

This is one area where parents create distrust and disappointment with their children. Children hang on to every word of the promises their parents make. A child has few things going on in his or her life, so when their parent(s) say they will do something, the child clings to the commitment the parent made. You as a parent have many other obligations going on that this one commitment to your child may not seem that important. Each time a commitment is broken, distrust and resentment builds. Over time, the child loses belief in what the parent has to say.

It is in the early years with your child that you build your "savings" account of trust so that when they go through their teenage years and begin to experience life through the influence of their peers that you can step in. It is at this point where you will either have a "savings account" of trust on which to draw on to help guide them through this time, or you will hear an argument from them with words like, *"Why should I listen to you? You told me so many times that you were going to do [fill in the blank] for me and never did. Why should I trust you now?"*

Fight Laziness
It is easy to be lazy.

I enjoy working out; I enjoy running. Yet, when the morning comes, even though I enjoy it, even though I know it is healthy for me, there is a part of me that wants to be lazy and not go to the gym.

If you look around, you see much from nature that demonstrates how important it is to shun laziness. Animals work during the spring, summer, and fall to prepare food for times when there will not be food.

Many of us struggle with the "0" years of our life; (ages 30, 40, 50, 60, 70...) because they are milestones that seem to force us to check our life's progress. The same is true on an annual basis with our birthday or New Year's. We look at the past, reflect on the dreams we had for our life, and wonder what happened. It takes a lot of courage for someone to look at their life at these moments and come to the conclusion that the reason they are where they are is because of the choices they made along the way. Those choices galvanized into habits.

I mentioned this before:

- sow a thought, reap an action
- sow an action, reap a habit
- sow a habit, reap a lifestyle
- sow a lifestyle, reap a destiny

Laziness can be a habit. We can talk ourselves into and out of many actions and justify the actions by saying we are too busy, that we need a break, we have worked hard all day, all week, all month, all year.

This laziness can come into play with your finances as well, meaning that before too long, you do not have a safety net or the financial liberty you want for your life. What if you developed a habit of putting away 5% or 10% of your income each month? The sooner you start, the more you have.

Be Careful of What You Say

If someone lies, or deceives others, what kind of a person would you think that person is? Is this someone you want around you? If they are willing to lie to others, what stops them from lying to you and looking for ways to take advantage of you? And if you associate with that person, people begin to link you as a friend of theirs; if they get into trouble, do not be naive and think for a moment that you are safe from the entanglement of their fall. You may be innocent of their deeds, but your reputation is in jeopardy because of your association with them.

A side note here for all of us who connect with "friends" or "associates" through social media sites: be careful who you connect with. Just because they are a "friend of a friend" does not mean they are someone to connect with. Some people want to tread on your good name for their benefit.

Seven deadly sins

Walking in Wisdom is full of counsel on how to identify what is right and what to avoid. These seven sins are the most obvious, and sometimes what is most obvious, we miss:

1. *Haughty eyes = Arrogance*
2. *Lying tongue = Liar*
3. *Hands that shed innocent blood = Fraud*

4. *Heart that develops wicked plans = Schemer*
   5. *Feet that run rapidly to evil = Instigator*
   6. *False witness who utters lies = Deceiver*
   7. *Spreads strife among brothers = Dissention*

It is easy to see these character traits in others; are any of these traits part of your life?

Fidelity is Not Just for Music

Our instruction in Walking in Wisdom comes from the loving father who wants to keep us safe, to protect us from the consequences of our actions, and to prevent us from making poor choices in the first place.

Observe the rules. To walk with them, bind them so they are with us when we sleep and when we wake up in the morning. Do not forsake wise instruction. All of this instruction is there to help us realize that what is good and right is really a lamp to light our way and guide us from error and evil.

One evil is sexual infidelity, both for the married and unmarried. It is simpler to understand why sexual fidelity in a marriage is important because of the marriage covenant. In the age we live in, sexual fidelity for those who are single is harder to appreciate.

How is a man seduced? The two most prevalent are by the words a woman speaks to him and the way in which she dresses. Men are visual. They become captivated by a woman's beauty. Men also have egos. They like the thrill of the hunt; in other words, that he still has what it takes to captivate and romance a woman. It is this conquest that leads a man down a path that makes him most vulnerable.

Also, what you do not know is that the woman you want to have an affair with may be more sinister than you think. All you may be to her is someone she can exploit, even blackmail. You may think this is a great mutual love, or something shared when you are out of town, only to find out that you are really her meal ticket.

Having an affair with a married person breaks trust and brings with it jealousy and vengeance. Avoiding an affair brings us back to Day Five of fleeing from temptation.

Day Seven
Avoid the Trap of Lust

Our instructor from Proverbs in Walking in Wisdom once again pleads with us to keep his words and treasure what he says; this is the idea of really living.

Freedom comes from a structured life.

If you have order in your life, you do not have to think about what you are going to do next. If you have made the decision to be healthy, eat well, and exercise, you do not have to keep questioning yourself if you should go to the gym each morning. You made that decision. Now it is a matter of keeping that commitment.

Remember, the more you do something, the more of a habit it becomes. *Your habits make you and then your habits keep you.*

The teacher from Proverbs wants us to keep wisdom as the apple of your eye, your most valuable treasure; write it on the tablet of your heart so you will not forget. Protect it like it is a loved one or a cherished friend who you would never betray.

Why? To keep you from straying into a life that brings heartache and death.

We hear a story about a young man who lacks sense and good judgment. This young man puts himself on the path of temptation because he goes out looking for sexual pleasure. He finds a woman in the darkness, where most of the deeds we want hidden happen.

Beware of your actions after the sun sets.

This woman is waiting for him. Trouble is always waiting for us. We think we are safe and will not get caught.

The woman is dressed to the nines, gregarious, fun to be around, and bold; she embraces him. When have you found some tempting offer to be dull, boring and unattractive?

She gives him reasons on why they will get away with the fun they will have and seduces him with the passion of desire and excitement; *"with her many persuasions she entices him; with her flattering lips, she seduces him".* *Proverbs 7:21*

Guess what he does? He follows her just like an ox to the slaughter.

My wife taught me a German phrase: *"MIT GEGANGEN, MIT GEFANGEN."* Its loose English translation is something like, *"you went along, now you are caught along."* I like to picture someone caught downstream in a boat, forced to go wherever the current takes him. This journey may cost you your life, your family, your career and everything you worked hard for. Is it worth it?

Choices

Our Proverbs teacher again pleads with the listener to pay attention to his words and not to let your heart turn aside to the ways of temptation. Do not stray onto the wrong path.

If not, you become another number, another victim seduced, destroyed, and cast down.

The house of temptation may look inviting from the outside, but the inside leads to destruction, descending down to the chambers of death.

Day Eight
Wisdom and Folly Contrasted

It is hard to comprehend that to find wisdom is not that difficult. It is all around us; speaking to us in many different ways.

Our teacher from Proverbs reminds us that wisdom itself, what some might call "common sense," is speaking to us all the time. It does not matter if we are in the grocery store, walking the malls, driving in our car, or at work.

It is the confirmation that there is nothing more valuable than wisdom; it is to be more highly desired than jewels and gems. Many scoff at this notion because we live in an age when money, power, fame, and influence bombard our thinking about what is important.

Where Does Wisdom Dwell
Wisdom dwells with prudence.

Prudence is the ability to govern and discipline oneself by using reason. It is being able to properly judge what is right and wrong and have the courage to make the right choices.

Wisdom is the enemy of pride, evil, and the perverted mouth. Pride characterized by arrogance, not pride based on self-respect, is what is meant here. Prideful arrogance sees no need for self-reflection and personal improvement.

Wisdom can put you in a position of authority and keep you there. Those who love wisdom and who diligently seek after her will find her. Also, there is a promise that the love of wisdom brings with it riches and honor as well as enduring wealth and righteousness.

This is something we do not understand; wisdom looks to endow those who love wisdom with wealth and fill their treasuries.

Wisdom from the Start

God possesses wisdom and from the beginning of time, He demonstrated His wisdom with the creation of all things. He delighted in wisdom, shouldn't we?

Blessing comes from obedience.

Hear and heed the instruction of wisdom. If you watch, wait, and listen during your daily activities, you will find instruction and direction; you will also find favor from the Lord.

The opposite is also true. If you neglect, miss the mark by ignoring wisdom, all you do is injure yourself. Those who hate wisdom, instruction, and guidance do not realize that they really love death (destruction) and have no one to blame but themselves for not listening.

Day Nine
The Table is Set

Our instructor from Proverbs creates an allegory about wisdom, likening it to a house. Wisdom, if a person, has built her house. A house with seven pillars. Seven is the number of completion, i.e. seven days in the week. This means that the dwelling place of wisdom is complete. The owner prepared her food, her drink, set the table, and sent out her maidens to call all those who want to partake in consuming what wisdom has to offer.

Contrasts of Behavior

How many times have you tried to help someone with gentle correction or instruction and ended up feeling humiliated for this attempt? Well, the instructor lets us know that if we attempt to correct a scoffer or reprimand a wicked man, we will receive dishonor and insults. The wicked person will insult us in an attempt to get us to back off. They are doing something wrong, they want to intimidate you for calling them out on their behavior. They want you to back down.

Those who are doing evil always look for ways to silence those who are exposing their deeds.

So if that happens, you know you are doing the

right thing in exposing them; continue doing so until the wrong is changed.

The opposite is true as well if someone who is teachable. Are you? If someone comes to correct you, do you embrace the correction? If so, you will become wiser still because you are teachable and are willing to listen.

Most of the time, people will keep to themselves and will not confront or correct someone. If someone does, it is usually because they care.

Those who rarely do this kind of "correction" are the ones you want to pay attention to.

There are those you meet who find fault in everyone. These people are easy to spot and their correction have limited value.

Once again we are reminded that all wisdom starts and ends with a fear of the Lord, a holy reverence for Him. Following along this path moves you in a direction of added years and increased number of days; the wiser you are, the more you keep yourself from foolish pursuits that can put you in harm's way.

Beware of the Woman of Folly

Here we are introduced to the woman of folly (foolishness, recklessness); it could be a man just the same.

The woman here is a contrast to the woman in the beginning of this chapter who illustrates wisdom by setting a table and inviting those seeking wisdom to dine with her.

Our woman of folly sits in a high prominent place of the city. This is a place that those who are foolish see as important (status, fame, position). She attempts to lure those who know what is right to compromise their integrity: ***"stolen water is sweet and bread eaten in secret is pleasant". Proverbs 9:17***

This thinking and behavior is really the beginning of a path to destruction. Advice is cheap. It reminds me of a story Zig Ziglar tells about the difference between a low price and a high cost of ownership. We are attracted to the low price and fail to consider the true cost of the purchase. The same holds true here. The advice is attractive, yet the cost of the advice makes all the difference.

Day Ten
Contrasts of Right and Wrong

Our teacher from Proverbs now moves into the contrasts between behaviors that are right verses wrong. Therefore the layout of the rest of the book follows this pattern.

The Proverbs of Solomon
1. Parenting is one of the toughest assignments in life. A child who is wise, who lives his or her life in a way that we have talked about so far, makes his other father glad; yet a foolish child is a grief to their mother. Why the difference here between a glad father and a grieving mother? A son carries on the father's name, and thus his son carries the fathers' ego and pride; so the father's character is on the line when his son goes out on his own. The same is true for a mother because mothers anguish emotionally over their children, knowing that foolish behavior results in hurt - hurt to themselves and hurt to others.

2. Those who seek to gain for the sake of gain will do so to the harm of others. Money and power obtained this way do not profit the person who is Walking in Wisdom. Righteousness can keep and,

thus, deliver the follower of wisdom from death (the things that lead to pain). Avoid people who use any means to get what they want.

3. How many people do you know that when they see a concert musician, a medal-winning athlete, an accomplished student, or a successful business person say that they are lucky? Those who are diligent - who pay the price of discipline, who practice and are dedicated are those who become outstanding. Those who are negligent or not willing to work hard, end up poor. They do not achieve what they set out to achieve and then want to compare their lives with those who they claim are "lucky".

4. History records the deeds of men and women, those who walk in righteousness. We remember them as a blessing to society. However, the names of the wicked are forever rotten in our memories. How do you want people to remember you?

5. You can notice those who are walking wisely. They are the ones who are sensitive to learning. They receive instruction well. The foolish are also easy to spot. They are the ones whose mouths

are always talking, almost babbling, and do not receive instruction well.

6. Consider these two people: one who carries himself with integrity in all his dealings, and the other carries himself in a way that is on the edge of honesty. Which of these two people will feel secure in their actions and which will be found out as a fraud?

7. The words you speak and what you talk about tells much about who you are. Those who are right in their walk are a fountain of life with the words they speak because they are producing what is positive. Just like clean water from a drinking fountain, they are refreshing. Those who are wicked in their walk use their mouth not as a fountain of life, but as a way to conceal their unkindness (or ways to take advantage of you) through the words they speak.

8. Hatred is the basis for all strife; it even stirs up strife when there is none. Love is the opposite. When love is the basis, one tends to forgive freely and is able to move on quicker instead of looking for reasons to have contention or hold onto bitterness.

9. How one talks is an indicator of what is going on in one's heart and mind. Those

who have discernment will find wisdom. Discernment means the willingness to look deeper into a subject. You may be hurt for rushing into something without doing your due diligence.

10. History shows us that having money is better than not having money because it provides a certain level of security and protection. The poor are the mercy of others to help them.

11. Just like in the Led Zeppelin song, *"Stairway to Heaven,"* there are two paths. The one who is on the path of life demonstrates this because they listen to instruction. I am sure you heard it asked about a person, "Is he teachable?" This means the person learns from his mistakes and is agreeable to instruction. Someone who forsakes listening to correction with the mindset or words that they "know" is the one who goes astray. It reminds me of raising my sons when they would say, *"I know,"* and I would respond that I know and I did are two different things. Saying you know something without backing it up with the right action means you really do not *"know it."*

12. What we say has the biggest impact on what happens to us. It can heal, help, or hurt our relationships. When was the last

time you were talking and said something only to regret it, realizing that if you had just shut up and did not say anything more, all would have been good? The more we say, chances are a problem will result. Those who are wise measure their words and control themselves from saying too much. It reminds me of the salesperson who, even after the client says yes to buying, continues to sell, only to find out that he just "sold" them out of the purchase by talking too much.

13. There are many today who struggle with whether it is right for a Christian to be rich. God's plan is to bless His children in many ways, financially being one of them. It is a blessing of the Lord that makes one rich, and the greater blessing is that He adds contentment with it. Many are rich, but feel miserable because they are unable to enjoy the blessing of their financial wealth.

14. Have you found that there are certain people who just seem to take pride in doing what is wrong? They see driving on the road as a race against other drivers and, therefore, cut people off, drive faster than the flow of traffic, and boast about how they can get to a location faster than someone else. They also behave this way in their business dealings. They see

it as a challenge if they can rip someone off or take advantage of someone just because they can. Then they put the blame on the other person for not being as "sharp" in business; or may something like "they get what they deserve for not being more aware." The one who is Walking in Wisdom is a man of understanding who takes pride in doing what is right. *"Doing wickedness is like sport to a fool and so is wisdom to a man of understanding." Proverbs 10:23*

15. Trust is a valuable possession, especially when you trust someone to go on your behalf and do work for you. Have you ever entered a smoke filled room and had your eyes sting and burn from the smoke? This is the same feeling you feel when you find out that the person you sent turns out to be lazy and unproductive.

16. Over time, we recognize that the one who speaks what is right is also the one who is wise. The opposite is also true. More often than not we see this manifested in business. Time reveals that those who are wicked and pervert the truth cannot be trusted.

Day Eleven

Contrast Between the Wise and the Foolish Continue

Day eleven of Walking in Wisdom is a continuation of the Teachers' contrasts.

1. How often is it easy to cheat? Everyone, at one time or another, is tempted by cheating. The teacher reminds us that God delights in doing what is right. That a *"false balance,"* in other words, cheating someone for your benefit is an abomination to God, but a *"just weight,"* doing what is fair to both the buyer and seller is His delight. Which side of the balance do you want to be on?

2. Those who are arrogant offend more people and therefore are not highly regarded; they are "dishonored" compared with those who are humble. If you are humble, chances are you are teachable. Being teachable leads to wisdom.

3. Like sailors of old who used the north star as their guide, we have a choice to use our integrity as our guide (which is a demonstration of doing what is right). This integrity means that no matter the

circumstances, we will stand for what is right. Those who are deceitful or two-faced, will drift back and forth between right and wrong. This can lead to disaster because a time will come when they will lie and deceive the wrong person. Choose to walk in integrity.

4. If you walk in a way that is blameless, in other words, where no one can accuse you of doing wrong, your walk will be smooth. I do not mean to say it will be effortless. There are people who will try to smear and malign you but you are at peace knowing that your heart and motives are right. The one who walks in a wicked way will fall by his own tricks and schemes. The more one does wrong, the greater the chance of falling. What are you doing that may cause your fall?

5. The godless man destroys his neighbor by using his mouth to lie and defraud him. However, the one who walks in the right way finds deliverance from this attack through knowledge. In other words, walking in wisdom means you are doing what is right and you will have a reputation that backs you up as well as others who will vouch for you and defend you.

6. When it goes well with those who do right in their efforts, everyone celebrates. Celebrating also takes place when players attempt to cheat or harm their opponent with cheap shots during a game. Are you taking cheap shots to give yourself an advantage?

7. The right leadership can make all the difference. If you do your work, lead others in the right way, and bless them with words of wisdom, fairness, and respect, it is no surprise to have success. If you use your mouth to deceive others, you create mistrust. How do you use your words at work, at home, and at play?

8. How many times have you shared your heart with someone and told them your pain, your plans, your dreams, your fears, only to find out they told someone else? Are you the kind of person who reveals secrets or are you trustworthy to conceal what someone shares with you? If the person wanted others to know, it is up to them to share it with others, right?

9. Some people have a hard time with order, with putting things in their place and having a plan on which to work from. They think it stifles them; they may even say they are just not that particular. If you have a playbook, a rule book, a way of

doing things, it will keep you from failing. Ray Kroc created the best franchise model with strict rules for managing McDonald's. This kind of guidance is a lesson for successful business building. If you have both wise guidance and trusted counselors, you will do well. What excuses are you making for not sticking to a process or guidance?

10. It is hard enough guaranteeing or vouching for someone you know. It is worse to do this for someone you barely know. The wise thing to do is help them figure out how they can build their reputation.

11. Everyone likes a woman who is gracious. Look at Princess Dianna. The world loved her because of who she was and the kindness she showed.

12. If you are merciful, you do yourself good; if you are cruel, you do yourself harm. When people testify in a trial, they will always give a good report about the one who treats others with mercy. Are you merciful and kind to all or are you cruel and unkind?

13. Everyone wants guarantees in life; we look for the seven steps, the ten ways...yet, principles stand the test of

time. If you do what is right, you will live longer than if you pursue a life that is filled with evil. The evil you do will trap you.

14. We live in a society where being discreet is no longer valued. *"As a ring of gold in a swine's snout, so is a beautiful woman who lacks discretion."* Proverbs 11:22

15. Generosity (and the increase in blessings that comes from it) is unexplainable. One is not generous so they can receive a blessing. One is generous because it is the right way to be. The opposite is also true. If one withholds what is right and justly due to someone, it will result in lack and want in one's life.

16. If you want favors from others, seek what is good for them; if you seek what is evil, evil will come your way. It is not complicated.

17. Your family trusts you. If you trouble them with your behavior or dishonor them with your actions, is it any wonder that you will not inherit anything? Is it any wonder that they will not trust you any longer?

Day Twelve
Attitude

1. Learning starts with attitude. Training for any sport or instrument takes discipline. If you love discipline, are willing to subject yourself to the training, you will excel. Knowledge comes the same way. If you dedicate yourself to a subject for 15-30 minutes a day, how much can you learn in a year? The person who hates to be corrected (also an attitude) displays that they are not teachable and therefore will remain foolish.

2. Every man (and woman) desires a faithful spouse. If they honor and respect their spouse, it is like a crown on their own head, like wearing expensive jewelry for all to see. If your spouse disrespects you (through adultery, mockery, physical abuse, disdain, contempt) then feelings of resentment make their way down into the deepest part of your being; it is like your body is decaying from the inside because of the pain you feel.

3. We judge others by their actions and their words. We give others praise by the insight they give and by what they contribute. If your mind focuses on what

you can take and not on what you can give, others will despise you.

4. There are those who puff themselves up by trying to impress others with what they have. The reality is that their demonstrated wealth maybe from credit card debt and living above their earnings. They look good, but they cannot afford to buy bread. It is better to be have less, live humbly and be genuine, than to live a lie and in debt.

5. To discern someone's character, watch how they treat their family members and pets. Do they treat them with compassion or cruelty?

6. There is a saying that the reason people do not accomplish all that they can is because they lack focus. If you focus on your task at hand you will have plenty. This is not the easy way; it takes hard work and effort. Yet, if you continually pursue what is easy, you lack good judgment. This too is another indicator of Walking in Wisdom. It is another way to evaluate which person makes a good associate and which one to avoid.

7. What we say has an impact on who we are and the success we have. Good words beget good, as do good deeds.

8. There is a fine line with determination, confidence, and drive because it can lead us into believing everything we say and do is correct. This false belief blinds us and leads us to foolish behavior and undesirable results. Yet, Walking in Wisdom seeks and listens to the counsel of others. If you do not have a "board of trustees" that you can go to with your ideas and your desired course of action, find them now. They will help guide your decision making.

9. One indicator to tell if someone is acting like a fool is by listening to what they share. Are they quick to share the depth and discomfort they feel from the problems they have, yet leave out what *they did* to get into the problem?

10. We must remember that Walking in Wisdom is recognizing the power of the words we speak. We can use harsh words, and they come across like sword thrusts, cutting deeply. Or we can use words to bring healing. Another indicator of someone Walking in Wisdom is the thoughtfulness they use in choosing the words they speak. Do you use your words to bring healing or hurting?

11. Lying is easy. Most of us get away with the lies we tell; when caught, there are

few physical or emotional consequences involved, so we keep lying. If you establish the practice of always telling the truth, you will understand that lying is only for a moment and has no redeeming quality. If you put yourself in a position of compromise, you put yourself in a position of having to lie in order to protect your ego and reputation. If you do not compromise, there is no need to lie.

12. Do you want to find delight in the Lord? Be faithful to what you say. Those who lie are an abomination to God. Trust is one of the purest and most precious things in this life. When you lie to the people who trust you, you are stealing from them. Once you cross the line and lie to someone, you are now capable of doing more and more harm to them.

13. A prudent man demonstrates carefulness and caution with his actions and what he says. He listens first and then decides what to say. If anything at all. The fool is the opposite. He will rush in to spout out words without thinking. Which one are you?

14. Do you want to work for others or have others work for you? Do you want to set your own wage or have others tell you what you can earn? If you work with a

diligent hand, others will work for you because you will either own your own business or be promoted to lead others. Put forth steady, sincere, and energetic effort. If not, you will work for someone else and have to settle for what others will pay you and not have the power, experience, or confidence to set your own wages.

15. It is hard for many of us to mask our feelings when we go through tough times. Anxiety in the heart weighs us down. A pleasant conversation makes the heart feel better. If you know someone who is suffering, share comforting and encouraging words.

16. A now retired basketball player was in a commercial in which he stated *"I'm not a role model"*. I beg to differ. We are all role models. The commercial may sell products but it does not tell the right message. The righteous is a guide to others. He is the right role model. When given a choice between the right path or the easy path, he chooses to take the right path. Those who chose to waffle between right and wrong based on what is expedient or convenient, will lead others astray.

17. You can enter someone's home, office, bedroom, or car and immediately tell if they are apathetic. If it is messy, dirty, or cluttered, chances are they will tell you they are not a neat freak, they are not compulsive about cleaning or they are super busy. My opinion is they are lazy and lack diligence. They chose to operate this way. However, *"the precious possession of a man (or woman) is diligence." Proverbs 12:27*
They will persist, they are meticulous, attentive, careful, and thorough.

Day Thirteen
Listening

1. One important characteristic of someone demonstrating wisdom is a person who accepts correction, who listens, and is coachable. Listening is learning. If you want to learn, then listen. The opposite is also true. Scoffers, when corrected, do not learn because they do not listen; they are busy mocking the person trying to help them.

2. Learnings' fruit is action. If you truly learn something, you put it into action. It becomes part of you.

3. If you are careful and mindful with what you say, you safeguard your life. The more you say that is uplifting and wise, the more good will come from it. The opposite is true, too. The more you say without discretion or discernment, the faster you will come to ruin.

4. The person who is a habitually lazy person (sluggard) craves for things they do not have. They complain that others are "lucky" because those people have what they want. The hard truth is that they are unwilling to do the necessary work for themselves to achieve what

those that they are envious of have. The opposite is also true; *"the soul of the diligent is abundantly satisfied." Proverbs 13:4*
The diligent (one characterized by steady, earnest, and energetic effort) is satisfied by what they achieve and for doing quality work. Which person are you?

5. Someone who desires to do what is right has a healthy understanding of right and wrong; he hates the lies and deception that people use to take advantage of others. But a wicked man has no problem acting disgustingly and shamefully, causing pain to others.

6. A quote I agree with says, *"our habits make us and then our habits keep us."* If we are Walking in Wisdom and practice what is right, this practice guards us to keep us on the right path, creating habits to help us make correct decisions. If you create habits based on just what feels good in the moment, you damage your integrity and you stumble.

7. How do you display what you gained materially in this life? There are those who pretend to be rich, but have nothing because debt created this facade. Then there are those who live modestly but have great wealth. John D. Rockefeller

and his wife Cettie are a great example. As their wealth grew, they continued to live modestly, choosing to give their money away, rather than using it to show off as their contemporaries did.

8. How do you make your decisions? Are you presumptuous, do you take liberties with the information you have, act rashly, overconfident, even arrogant? This attitude will lead to strife, conflict, and poor decisions. However, if you submit yourself to the counsel of others, you can make more wise decisions because others may know more about the subject, will present a different perspective, or may even have had to make the same decision you are making.

9. Most people want to increase their income. If obtained by fraud, it will dwindle or go away. Those who increase their income by cheating others look for the quick fix or fast play and do not have the appreciation for the hard work it takes to make money, nor the self-control to keep it. If you increase your income and accumulate your wealth through hard work, your income increases because you work hard at keeping what you earned.

10. *"Hope deferred makes the heart sick. But desire fulfilled is a tree of life."*

Proverbs 13:12
Do you want to destroy the trust of your child? Continue to promise to do something with them or for them, and keep putting it off and telling them (and yourself), that you are too busy, that you are sorry, that you will make it up to them or that something came up (that is more important in your mind). We do this to people as well, but since children idolize us, and it is easier for them to trust us, it hurts them more. We teach them through this action that we cannot be trusted and we are not a person of our word. How do you feel when what you wanted, what you desire, is fulfilled? It is like a "tree of life." You are full of energy. Your child (or spouse) acts (and feels) the exact same way.

11. Who do you receive your instruction from? If you seek out those who are wise, it leads to a fountain of life, spiritual vitality, and energy. It guides you by helping you to turn away from what causes you harm.

12. The more you know, the more benefit you can have in any given situation. If you use knowledge correctly, you bring information that is helpful.

13. If you want to learn from a man who is practical, sensible, farsighted, then watch

what he does. He acts with knowledge, meaning he gathers the facts, the right information, becomes aware, and seeks to understand before taking action. The opposite is also true. Those who are foolish display their folly by doing just the opposite and then wondering (and complaining) that the action they took did not bring the results they expected.

14. What kind of a messenger are you? Are you the faithful one who, when asked to deliver a message, does it to the best of your ability? If so, you bring healing to the situation because you are a trusted person. Or are you the person who gets distracted when you hear the message? Or do you embellish or remove words from the message you are to deliver because you think it is a better that way? Regardless of your opinion, do what you are asked to do and deliver the message as it was given to you.

15. *"Poverty and shame come to him who neglects discipline. But he who regards reproof receives honor." Proverbs 13:18*
We talked about this before. There are too many examples of people who are unwilling to live in a manner of self-control and discipline and it leads to their ruin. Drugs, alcohol, gambling, and promiscuous sex, are a few of the

undisciplined habits that come to mind. If you are already involved, seek help to break the shackles that are leading you to poverty and shame. You can overcome. God is stronger than your temptation. Take action now. If you regard reproof, you will receive honor, which means you can protect your good name and reputation.

16. *"Desire realized is sweet to the soul, but it is an abomination to fools to depart from evil." Proverbs 13:19*
How wonderful it is when what you worked hard for, or desired, happens. Yet for those who act in a way that lacks judgment, it is difficult and even strange for them to depart from their evil ways to pursue something desirable.

17. I heard it once said that whoever you associate with for a three year period, you will rise to their level of income, knowledge, and morals. *"He who walks with wise men will be wise, but the companion of fools will suffer harm." Proverbs 13:20*
Who are your companions and what kind of people do you associate with?

18. Over the course of one's life, many people tend to move from the pursuit of gaining wealth to wanting to leave a legacy. They

realize that the legacy they leave for their children and grandchildren has more of an impact than what they financially accumulated. ***"A good man leaves an inheritance to his children's children." Proverbs 13:22***
What are you leaving for yours?

19. Those who are poor end up being the ones most taken advantage of. Even though they have the willingness to work hard, there are those who use political means to figure out ways to take what the poor have away from them.

20. We live in a western society that has moved away from consequences for bad behavior. I heard college football coach Bobby Bowden speak at a Fellowship of Christian Athletes Fiesta Bowl breakfast, and he shared this observation. Someone asked him if the student-athlete has changed over the past 40 years since he started coaching. He said no, they have not. The players are typical young men in their late teens and early twenties with the same kinds of drives, desires, and ambitions. He said that what has changed is the parents and parenting. He said more and more parents neglect proper discipline and consequences for their children's bad behavior, which leads to self-centered behavior as adults.

Day Fourteen
Belief

1. Temperaments create a home environment that either build up or tear down. The temperament of a woman is one that creates the most influence because most men (husbands) will defer to wanting to make their wife happy, happy wife = happy life. Therefore, a wise woman understands this and a foolish one does not. The wise woman works to keep a home tranquil and make it a haven of protection for her family. The foolish one does not make such efforts.

2. There is a certain reality that if someone has a reverence and belief in God, they will walk in a way that benefits others. Those who do not have a fundamental belief in God have no check on their behavior. Interviews of criminals who committed serious violent crimes determined they did not have a belief in God. They may change through prison ministries, but their actions prior to being arrested and imprisoned demonstrates a disregard for others and the law.

3. What we say has consequences. If I speak foolishly (without thinking about the words I use), I set myself up for

repercussions. *"In the mouth of the foolish is a rod for his back, but the lips of the wise will protect them." Proverbs 14:3*
If you are wise in what you say, chances are you will not have unforeseen consequences and repercussions.

4. *"Where no oxen are, the manger is clean, but much revenue comes by the strength of the ox." Proverbs 14:4*
   The idea with this proverb is that you do not have to worry about cleaning your barn if you have no oxen. If you want revenue, you need oxen. No oxen, no mess, no revenue. If you want to accomplish much, it requires change, and you will have new challenges to work through, but the rewards are great.

5. Lying is the easiest of vices. It started at creation. We see children at a young age lying about their behavior. As a parent, you see one child hit another child; you confront the child and ask him if he hit the child, and what is his answer? No. Yet, *"a trustworthy witness will not lie, but a false witness utters lies." Proverbs 14:5*
   Honesty is a choice; so is lying.

6. Our attitude determines our accomplishments. *"A scoffer (one who mocks or ridicules) seeks wisdom and*

finds none." Proverbs 14:6
Why? Because they do not believe they benefit from other people's counsel. They have all the answers. *"But knowledge is easy to one who has understanding."* If you want to live by this principle, knowledge comes by hearing; you need to listen to gain understanding.

7. *"Leave the presence of a fool, or you will not discern words of knowledge." Proverbs 14:7*
   Who you associate with influences you. The more you associate with those who lack judgment in their decision making, the more you will lose your ability to judge properly.

8. Another way to measure if someone is Walking in Wisdom is to find out if he or she is a person who seeks to understand why he/she does what they do, why others do what they do, and what he/she can learn from all the events in his/her life. The foolish person deceives himself by telling himself this kind of evaluation is unimportant.

9. Another indicator of the person Walking in Wisdom is their attitude toward right and wrong.

10. No one can really know the depths of our pain. They may say they do. They may have gone through a similar experience, but they really cannot fully comprehend the depths of our emotions. We need to remember this, too, when we try to comfort someone. The same is true about the heights of joy one feels. Here, too, be careful and avoid judging someone who is unable to share the same level of joy you do. Also avoid feeling bad if you are unable to enter into someone else's level of joy.

11. Self-reliance, arrogance, and over confidence makes us believe the course of action we are taking is the right one, but its end is disaster. *"There seems a way which seems right to a man, but its end is the way of death." Proverbs 14:12* Protect yourself and seek wise counsel.

12. Outward appearance is not the best way to know how someone is feeling. They may be laughing and in good cheer on the outside, but their heart may be in pain. Also, even in celebration, there can be over indulgence which leads to problems. *"Even in laughter the heart may be in pain, and the end of joy may be grief." Proverbs 14:13*

13. Those who go back on their commitments justify and rationalize their actions. Those who keep their commitments are pleased with their actions and rationalize their choices, too. *"The backslider in heart will have his fill of his own ways, but a good many will be satisfied with his." Proverbs 14:14*

14. *"The naïve believes everything, but the sensible man considers his steps." Proverbs 14:15*
Need I say more?

15. *"A wise man is cautious and turns away from evil, but a fool is arrogant and careless." Proverbs 14:16*
The contrast here is striking. Those who are arrogant believe they have all the answers and, therefore, end up making careless decisions. This confirms their foolishness. Yet, the wise man is cautious, and because he is cautious is able to turn away from what can bring him harm.

16. Have you come across someone who is quick tempered? Another term might be someone whose buttons are easily pushed. This person is a slave to his emotions. He acts rashly, without thinking. This kind of behavior is costly to relationships.

17. It is fascinating how people gravitate to those who are rich and avoid those who are poor. The rich have something we want (money), and we have this belief that by befriending them, we will gain something. Since the poor do not have the money to do this, we actually look down on them and avoid befriending them. *"The poor is hated even by his neighbor, but those who love the rich are many." Proverbs 14:20*

18. Someone asked Jesus, "who is my neighbor?" Jesus then went on and told the story of the Good Samaritan. *"He who despises his neighbor sins, but happy is he who is gracious to the poor." Proverbs 14:21*
We always seem to find it easier to help those who can "pay us back" when we help them. Helping those who cannot return the favor feeds the soul.

19. I heard it said once that the more energy you put into something, the more it will grow. I think there is an element of truth to that. *"In all labor there is profit, but mere talk leads only to poverty." Proverbs 14:23*
There is a big difference between talking about doing something and actually doing something. Ben Franklin said, *"Well done is better than well said."*

20. As a father, we want to protect our children. If you live your life based on faith in God, trusting in His providence for your life, and live to pass this on to your children, you will give them a great gift of protection. *"In the fear (reverence) of the Lord there is strong confidence, and his children will have refuge."*
Proverbs 14:26

21. The more I cling to the Lord and respect Him as my Creator, the more faith I have in His divine plan for my life. This gives me energy and life, like a fountain of water. This respect/reverence also protects me because there is a set of standards by which I live my life that keep me from what can harm me. *"The fear of the Lord is a fountain of life, that one may avoid the snares of death."*
Proverbs 14:27

22. How we deal with our anger is of great importance. If we take the time to calm ourselves, we can better evaluate the situation to make better choices with our actions. The opposite is true too; if we are quick-tempered, we act foolishly *"He who is slow to anger has great understanding, but he who is quick-tempered exalts folly."*
Proverbs 14:29

23. Those who are prone to extreme emotional swings or are unable to manage their emotions have more physical problems than those who have tempered their emotions. We all have emotions. How do you manage yours? *"A tranquil heart is life to the body, but passion is rottenness to the bones." Proverbs 14:30*
The passion mentioned above is not the passion having high energy for something. It is about uncontrolled emotion.

24. Some people find it easy to take advantage of those who are poor. Be careful if you do this. *"He who oppresses the poor taunts his Maker, but he who is gracious to the needy honors Him." Proverbs 14:31*

25. *"Righteousness exalts a nation, but sin is a disgrace to any people." Proverbs 14:34*
There is truth to this principle. It starts in the home; if you set the tone of your home to do what is right, then chances are your children will do what is right. If parents have no regard for right and wrong, is it any wonder that their children do not either?

26. More times than not, if you do well in your service at work, you will benefit from it. If you act in a way that brings shame to your employer, chances are you will not remain there. *"The king's favor is toward a servant who acts wisely, but his anger is toward him who acts shamefully." Proverbs 14:35*

Day Fifteen
The Words You Use

1. Here is another reminder of the power of what we say and how we say it. How many times have you reacted to a situation only to regret it, even moments later? You can never take back what you said or how you said it. Those words and how you delivered the message actually inflamed the situation instead of bringing about resolution. *"A gentle answer turns away wrath, but a harsh word stirs up anger." Proverbs 15:1*

2. Why are some teachers and coaches so influential in a person's life? It is because the good ones make us thirsty to learn, hunger to do more, to be better. *"The tongue of the wise makes knowledge acceptable, but the mouth of fools spouts folly." Proverbs 15:2*

3. A person's character is all about who they are when no one is looking. It is easy to be "good" when you have someone watching you; many studies lately show how people's behavior changed when they thought someone was watching them. *"The eyes of the Lord are in every place, watching the evil and the good." Proverbs 15:3*

4. What do conmen use to dupe their subjects? Their words. The same words that can bring healing and help with sincerity by provoking feelings of trust are also available to take advantage of someone who is hurting and vulnerable. *"A soothing tongue is a tree of life, but perversion in it crushes the spirit." Proverbs 15:4*

5. As a father, we try to help our children realize that what we share with them is for their own good. It could be that we suffered the consequences of poor choices that we made or can see down the road to the end results of poor choices. I heard it said…"Little children, little problems; big children, bigger problems." Most of us learn the hard way. *"A fool rejects his father's discipline, but he who regards reproof is sensible." Proverbs 15:5*

6. Most of the time, successful people are willing to share what they learned and are willing to help others who are striving accomplish more. *"The lips of the wise spread knowledge, but the hearts of fools are not so." Proverbs 15:7*

7. We cannot earn our way into God's favor. God's favor comes through faith alone in Jesus Christ alone. Jesus said in the

Sermon on the Mount, *"blessed are those who hunger and thirst for righteousness, for they shall be satisfied."* Solomon said, ***"The way of the wicked is an abomination to the Lord, but He loves one who pursues righteousness." Proverbs 15:9***

8. When we experience joy, it shows in our appearance; our face reflects it. When our heart is sad, we tend to come across with a broken spirit and low energy. ***"A joyful heart makes a cheerful face, but when the heart is sad, the spirit is broken." Proverbs 15:13***
Sometimes we just cannot "manufacture" a happy face when we are depressed. If you see someone who does not seem happy to you, be mindful of how you approach them. They may have a hurting heart. You can do much to help them with a word of encouragement or sincerely asking them how they are doing.

9. How many people have you come across that no matter what you say, they find something to complain about it? ***"All the days of the afflicted are bad, but a cheerful heart has a continual feast." Proverbs 15:15***

10. We live in a society of "going big or going home" - the drive to strive to have more. There is great satisfaction in setting goals

and achieving them. God made us this way. However, God's plan is for us to be content and to enjoy the blessings we have, no matter how great or how meager. What we have, especially in North America and most western countries, far exceeds what others have who were not blessed to be born here. *"Better is a little with the fear of the Lord than great treasure and turmoil with it and Better is a dish of vegetables where love is than a fattened ox served with hatred." Proverbs 15:16*

11. Two people find themselves in a volatile situation. One is quick to judge and engages his emotions; the other takes an investigative approach and keeps his emotions in check. Which of the two will navigate to a better end? *"A hot-tempered man stirs up strife, but the slow to anger calms a dispute." Proverbs 15:18*

12. I grew up near a creek, and around the creek was a forest with thick underbrush of briars. We would play hide and seek, army, and tag through the woods. The last thing you wanted to do was make a wrong turn and end up in the briar patch. The same is true for someone who is lazy. They are given a task to do and by not doing it, they find themselves always

playing catch up and never getting ahead. *"The way of the lazy is as a hedge of thorns, but the path of the upright is a highway." Proverbs 15:19*

13. Do you want to be successful? Seek wise counsel. *"Without consultation, plans are frustrated, but with many counselors they succeed." Proverbs 15:22* Look back over the plans you had and study what worked and what did not. Study the lives of those who are successful, and you will find that they all had others that they went to for advice as a sounding board. Now it is also important to be wise in who you go to for advice. If you want a successful marriage, visit with those who have a successful marriage. If you want a thriving business, meet with people whose business is prosperous.

14. It is a great feeling when what you say makes all the difference to someone, right? *"A man has joy in an apt answer, and how delightful is a timely word!" Proverbs 15:23*

15. No man (or woman) is an island. What you do has consequences to those around you, especially your family. *"He who profits illicitly (illegally, dishonestly) troubles his own house, but he who hates*

bribes will live." Proverbs 15:27
If you turn away from compromising your character for money, chances are you will spare your household from trouble and set an example for your children to do the same.

16. How do you begin each day? Each of us have challenges in our lives; it is still our choice on how we let them affect us. *"Bright eyes gladden the heart; Good news puts fat on the bones." Proverbs 15:30*

17. Some say that there are two ways we change; either from within yourself, at your choosing, or outside yourself, at someone else's choosing. *"He who neglects discipline despises (looks down on) himself, but he who listens to reproof acquires understanding." Proverbs 15:32*
Discipline is another word for setting boundaries. We all make excuses. *"I tried that before, and it did not work for me,"* is really saying that I am unable to believe in myself. Those who are willing to listen to reproof no matter how painful it is, learn from this, gain understanding, and if wise, make a correction in their behavior.

Day Sixteen
Our Activity - God's Outcome

1. We think we have all the answers. We detail the steps of our plans and then forget that the Lord is really the one who determines what the results will be.

2. We are quick to judge others but not so quick to judge ourselves the same way. Jesus taught the disciples in the Sermon on the Mount to first take the log out of their own eye before trying to take the splinter out of their neighbor's eye. We think we are alright and work to convince others of the same. Yet only God knows the true motives of our heart and our true character. If you want to measure yourself, use Christ as your measure.

3. If you want peace in your decisions, turn over your efforts to the Lord. It is an act of faith to believe that what we do and what happens in our life happens because of God's plan for our life. It is time to rest in this belief. *"Commit your works to the Lord and your plans will be established." Proverbs 16:3*

4. When someone loves you, forgiveness follows when you mess up. When you love someone, you work to keep from

messing up. *"By loving-kindness and truth, iniquity is atoned for, and by the fear of the Lord one keeps away from evil." Proverbs 16:6*

5. *"When a man's ways are pleasing to the Lord, He makes even his enemies to be at peace with him." Proverbs 16:7*
This tells us that those who follow after righteousness and act with kindness, will still have enemies, but the unseen hand of God directs your enemies to be at peace with you.

6. Once again, our instruction is to understand that *"it is better to have a little with righteousness, than great income with injustice." Proverbs 16:8*

7. *"The mind of man plans his ways, but the Lord directs his steps." Proverbs 16:9*
The bible tells the story of Jonah who thought he could run from the Lord's instruction to preach repentance to the city of Nineveh. He took passage on a ship, and the ship began to sink because of a great storm; Jonah jumped into the water and a great fish swallowed him. The fish spit him out on the beach three days later to do what his original assignment was: preach repentance to the city of Nineveh. We can devise all the plans we want, yet God is the one who

makes happen what He wants to have happen. History is really His story.

8. Being just and fair is a choice. It is a decision. God concerns himself with us being honest in our business dealings. ***"A just balance and scales belong to the Lord; all the weights of the bag are His concern." Proverbs 16:11***

9. Leadership is a great responsibility. People look up to those in leadership and follow their direction. ***"It is an abomination for kings to commit wickedness, for a throne is established on righteousness." Proverbs 16:12***

10. Leaders who speak what is right bring delight to those who work for them and therefore earn their love and respect.

11. Remember that those who are in a leadership role have the power to make or break your success. If you anger them, you do not know the consequences. However, if you are wise in what you say to them or about them, you will avoid their anger.

12. I heard it said that whatever you want *"is either owned or controlled by someone else."* If you receive that person's favor, you will get what you want.

13. Benjamin Franklin said, *"an investment in knowledge always pays the best interest."* ***"How much better it is to get wisdom than gold! And understanding is to be chosen above silver." Proverbs 16:16***

14. A highway allows you to travel faster. If you depart from doing wrong you are on a highway of doing what is right. You are diligent watching the way you live your life in order to keep you safe from harm.

15. ***"Pride goes before destruction, and a haughty spirit before stumbling." Proverbs 16:18***
    This is a reminder to check with counselors before venturing off on your own decisions.

16. The more you grow in wisdom, the more your reputation spreads as one who is discerning (perceptive, sharp, discriminating). And the more you prefect the sweetness of what you speak, the more persuasive you become.

17. The more knowledge and understanding you have, the more resources you have at your disposal. You are less able to be deceived and, thus, taken advantage of.

18. Those walking in wisdom are always learning. They teach themselves what is right to say because they know that words

have power to change lives and situations. By taking this approach, you can add persuasiveness (influence, eloquence, expressiveness) to your speaking.

19. *"Pleasant words are a honeycomb, sweet to the soul and healing to the bones." Proverbs 16:24*
Nothing to add here about the power of our words.

20. We have to be ever mindful that what we think is the right way to go may lead to destruction. *"There is a way which seems right to a man, but its end is the way of death." Proverbs 16:25*
This is so critical today when we have the media, internet, peers, pundits, and frauds all looking to peddle their beliefs and opinions. *"If you don't stand for something, you will fall for anything."* - Abraham Lincoln.

21. *"A worker's appetite works for him, for his hunger urges him on." Proverbs 16:26*
This is not just the hunger for food but the desire to achieve your goals and dreams. Hard work is profitable.

22. Another check point of who not to associate yourself with: *"A worthless (empty) man digs up evil, while his words*

are as a scorching fire." Proverbs 16:27
Someone who goes about looking for what is wrong and uses his words to hurt others is someone to avoid.

23. Another characteristic to look out for is someone who spreads strife or looks to create dissention, particularly in the form of someone who talks behind your back. This behavior often times separates close friends.

24. Have you been around a group of friends who pressure you (or others) to do something? This is peer pressure and it happens all the time, no matter your age. More times than not, this pressuring is not for something good: it leads you in a way that is not to your benefit.

25. Self-control is a great character trait. It is one of the Fruit of the Spirit. *"He who is slow to anger is better than the mighty, and he who rules over his spirit than he who captures a city." Proverbs 16:32* Alexander the Great died from his excessiveness, his lack of self-control, at the age of 32. History tells us that Alexander indulged heavily in drinking parties, often over days and nights. He competitively out drank those around him.

26. We may think we are participating in games of chance, but all outcomes are from the Lord. *"The lot is cast into the lap, but its every decision is from the Lord." Proverbs 16:33*
This is not an endorsement for gambling. It is a reminder that when someone says, "you're lucky," they do not understand God's blessing.

Day Seventeen
Justice

1. A number of years ago I ate a dry bowl of cereal for breakfast. Why this meant so much to me is that I let someone else finish off the milk. I felt good knowing that I did not have to think about drinking the last of the milk and them having to do without. This verse is about comparing having little to eat and being at peace (no milk) verses much feasting (a banquet of food) but with violent conflict. *"Better is a dry morsel and quietness with it, than a house full of feasting with strife." Proverbs 17:1*

2. There are times when the owner of a company will treat one of his workers better than one of his children. This is especially true if the worker acts wisely. When the owner wants to retire, chances are he will trust this worker with his business more than his own child because the child did not display the same kind of sound decision making.

3. Purity makes things more valuable. *"Gold is tried in the furnace and silver in a refining pot to take the dross out and make the metal more precious."*

Proverbs 17:3
We are no different. God, using circumstances that are outside of our control, tests our hearts to show us what kind of character we have. What is on the inside always makes its way to the outside.

4. Man has not changed much over the years; some still mock those who are poor (or homeless) with an attitude that there is something wrong with them for being that way. There are also people who celebrate when problems come into people's lives.

5. You will not find a fool speaking like one who is wise; just like you do not want or expect to hear lying coming from someone in a leadership role.

6. There are some who think that they do well by bribing others. All it does is create a false sense of accomplishment and arrogance. The day will come when someone does not accept the bribe.

7. If we are friends and you forgive me for something I do wrong to you and then I do it again, would this behavior make our friendship better, or would you feel it is pulling us apart? *"He who covers a transgression seeks love, but he who*

repeats a matter separates intimate friends." Proverbs 17:9

8. Those who Walk in Wisdom understand that correction is an important way to learn because it puts us back on the right path. Those who do not care or see the value in learning, will not learn. It is not important to them. You can lead a horse to water, but you cannot make it drink.

9. It is more dangerous for you to be around someone who is acting foolishly than to be around a mother bear robbed of her cubs. The bear is interested in protecting her little ones. The fool is unpredictable, and you have no idea what he will do and, therefore, how it will affect you.

10. *"He who returns evil for good, evil will not depart from his house." Proverbs 17:13* If you are ungrateful to people for the good they show you and repay them with evil, it is reasonable to expect someone may take revenge on you for this behavior.

11. Little disagreements lead to big arguments. Nip it in the bud before it gets too far. *"The beginning of strife is like letting out water, so abandon the quarrel before it breaks out." Proverbs 17:14*

12. God reminds us that He hates those who justify the behavior of the wicked. God also hates those who condemn people who are doing what is right.

13. When times are tough is when you find out who your friends are and how close your relatives are. *"A friend loves at all times, and a brother is born for adversity." Proverbs 17:17*
How do you react when those around you are in trouble and need help?

14. It is poor judgment to become a co-signer for someone else because you put yourself in jeopardy if the person you co-sign for does not pay.

15. *"A joyful heart is good medicine, but a broken spirit dries up the bones." Proverbs 17:22*
Think about the times when you are around someone who is always pleasant to be around. They are upbeat and it makes you feel upbeat. There are those who are miserable. We do not know the reason. It may be because of circumstances. It may be a habit of seeing the glass as "half empty." Either way, it makes you feel worse by being around them.

16. Parents want the best for their children; this does not mean only financially. I say that most parents are ok if their children were less "successful" financially, provided they made the right choices for their life. *"A foolish son is a grief to his father, and bitterness to her who bore him." Proverbs 17:25*

17. If you reward the behavior displayed, chances are you will receive more of it. *"It is not good to fine the righteous, nor to strike the noble for their uprightness." Proverbs 17:26*
If you punish those who do good, what incentive is there for others to do good?

18. *"He who retains his words has knowledge, and he who has a cool spirit is a man of understanding. Even a fool, when he keeps silent, is considered wise; when he closes his lips, he is considered wise." Proverbs 17:27*
There is a saying I like that goes something like this, "it is better to keep your mouth closed and have others think that you are wise than to open your mouth and speak just to have all doubt of you being wise removed."

Day Eighteen
Trust

1. If you refuse to seek counsel, you separate yourself from the opportunity of sound wisdom.

2. Another check point for those Walking in Wisdom: does the person you are with find enjoyment in learning and growing, or just in revealing what he knows and hearing himself brag about himself?

3. Sometimes the hardest way to communicate is to be simple in your explanation. Some people make even the simplest things seem complicated just by how they explain them.

4. Fairness is what everyone wants. Everyone can be fair; it is a choice. To show partiality is wrong, especially to those who are unfair.

5. The fool opens his mouth and produces conflict, discord, dissention, and fighting; he just does not realize that what he says is a trap for his own soul. What he gives, he will receive.

6. Be careful around people who speak with subtleties or use words in a cutting, sarcastic way, and then say they were just

joking. They may try to say that you took what they said the wrong way or that you are overly sensitive. The words they speak go down deep into your soul, and they tend to fester. You cannot seem to get rid of them, and you second guess yourself as if you are the one who is in the wrong.

7. A person you hire and trust because of their commitment to do quality work will undermine your reputation if they fail to perform. It can lead to the destruction of your company.

8. When times get tough, those who trust in the Lord find Him to be a safe tower; they have no shame in trusting Him.

9. Money has a tendency to give us a false sense of protection; it can take care of a lot of problems, but it can also leave us as quickly as it came.

10. Many times when a person fails at something or something goes terribly wrong, it is because they are arrogant. Think about these situations while driving: you text, talk on the phone, or maybe eat. All are distractions that last a few seconds. Those few seconds are enough to cause an accident that can kill or maim someone for life. We are so arrogant that

we believe that we can "multi-task," are in control, and nothing bad will happen. Done enough times, our actions become habits and we no longer stop to think there might be a problem. *"Before destruction the heart of man is haughty, but humility goes before honor." Proverbs 18:12*

11. Have you found yourself thinking you know what someone is going to say, so you interrupt them to give your input, only to find out you were completely wrong? *"He who gives an answer before he hears, it is folly and shame to him." Proverbs 18:13*

12. Hope makes all the difference. When one is sick, if he has hope, he will endure the sickness; if he does not have hope, then he cannot bear the burden to fight on.

13. *"The mind of the prudent acquires knowledge, and the ear of the wise seeks knowledge." Proverbs 18:15* Both are action oriented; both the prudent person and the wise find knowledge as something to pursue.

14. There is a difference in giving a gift and giving a bribe. They both may have the same monetary value, yet the intent in which you give them have two different

purposes. A gift is only a true gift if given with no expectation. A gift becomes a bribe when it is given or promised in order to influence the judgment or conduct of a person in a position of trust.

15. *"The first to plead his case seems just, until another comes and examines him." Proverbs 18:17*
It is best to gather all the facts before making a judgment.

16. When there is dissention because of disagreement on a decision, sometimes it is better to come to an answer by flipping a coin then to continue arguing and making no progress.

17. When you offend someone with your behavior, it is harder to win them back than it is to win over a city of people who you have never had contact with. The more contention you have with someone, the more you build a wall that separates you from that person.

18. We earn our livelihood with what we say:
"With the fruit of a man's mouth his stomach is satisfied; he will be satisfied with the product of his lips." Proverbs 18:20

19. What you and I say have the power to give or to take life; we either build up and encourage or tear down and discourage.

20. The poor in spirit will inherit the earth; they are the ones who pray to God for enrichment. They are humble before God and to others even though they may be wealthy. Some monetary rich people have a different mindset. They speak harshly to others because they think their wealth makes them more important.

21. The more friends you have, the more opportunity for you to get into trouble. Be mindful of who you have as your friends because true friends are few.

Day Nineteen
Integrity

1. It is better to have your integrity and be poor than be someone who uses his words and influence to take advantage of others and also acts like a fool.

2. There is a phrase *"haste makes waste"*; ***"Also, it is not good for a person to be without knowledge, and he who makes haste with his feet errs." Proverbs 19:2*** It is a mistake to take action before considering the consequences.

3. It is funny how we make foolish decisions, and when it brings about consequences we do not want, we then blame God for our misfortunes.

4. Do you want many friends? If you become wealthy you will see how many people want to be your friend. Want to lose those same friends? Suffer the loss of your money and see how many stick around.

5. ***"Those who go about as a liar will not escape; they are always found out." Proverbs 19:5***

6. *"Many will entreat the favor of a generous man, and every man is a friend to him who gives gifts."* Proverbs 19:6

7. *"He who gets wisdom loves his own soul; he who keeps understanding will find good."* Proverbs 19:8

8. *"A man's discretion gives him the understanding to not react with anger and to overlook a wrong doing."* Proverbs 19:11

9. Our family can bring us comfort and encouragement, or they can be a place of strife and agony. *"A foolish son is destruction to his father, and the contentions of a wife are a constant dripping."* Proverbs 19:13

10. If you have a prudent wife, it is a true gift from the Lord. We think we really know someone during the engagement process. Many of us do not do enough to really get to know our future spouse during the dating/engagement process. During this process, are you willing to postpone the marriage or even end the relationship if you see that the relationship is not healthy? If not, a hurting marriage and then a painful divorce may be waiting at the end.

11. Laziness is a habit that casts a long shadow. The more you allow laziness to creep into your life, the more it takes over. Its effect is like being in a deep sleep that you cannot wake up from.

12. A life with a code of conduct is one that keeps you from harm; if you are careless with your habits and behaviors, you will suffer harm. You may even die early because of the lifestyle you chose.

13. God's plan is for people to take care of people, not for government programs to take care of people. *"He who is gracious to the poor man lends to the Lord and He will repay him for his good deed." Proverbs 19:17*

14. It is best to correct and discipline your children when they are in their pre-teen years to establish right from wrong as this is when they are most impressionable. It is also a time to build a relationship with them that indicates that you care about them and have their best interest in mind. If you do not do this, a time may come where their rebellion will cause you and your family much pain.

15. It is futile to rescue a man given to angry outbursts because his temper will repeatedly land him in trouble. It does not

mean you should not try; just be aware of how often it happens.

16. There is no time like the present to gain wisdom. *"Listen to counsel and accept discipline that you may be wise the rest of your days."* Proverbs 19:20

17. We come up with so many ideas, so many plans, and so many dreams; it is the ones that you take to the Lord in prayer and then gain peace with that are the ones to pursue.

18. *"What is desirable in a man is his kindness; it is better to be a poor man than a liar."* Proverbs 19:22
Isn't this the kind of person you want to be and want to be around?

19. A clear conscience creates a good night's sleep. There is peace in ones' heart knowing he is doing what is right in God's eyes. He understands God's plan for him, he walks in it, and has faith that God has his back. Therefore, he can rest easy each night with this trust in the Lord.

20. The trouble with certain kinds of punishment is that they only make the one who committed the crime more shrewd. It actually makes it harder to catch them the next time. Yet if you reprove someone who has understanding that they did

something wrong, they will gain knowledge that this behavior is wrong and not repeat the offense.

21. *"Cease listening my son to discipline, and you will stray from the words of knowledge." Proverbs 19:27*
If you become soft on yourself and neglect your code of conduct, over time you will gravitate to the things that before you would not do.

Day Twenty
Be Prepared

1. Drinking alcohol is a large part of our society. It is a social rite of passage when a person turns 18 or 21, depending on state laws. There is peer pressure to drink at parties. The consequences from being intoxicated create more problems, yet the next weekend, most are back at it. *"Wine is a mocker, strong drink a brawler, and whoever is intoxicated by it is not wise."* Proverbs 20:1

2. Those in authority receive respect because of their position; if you provoke them to anger, you take into your own hands the consequences of provoking them.

3. It takes more character to have self-control than to get into a fight. *"Keeping away from strife is an honor for a man, but any fool will quarrel."* Proverbs 20:3

4. Those who are lazy find all sorts of reasons why their work is not completed. Then they complain and look for help from others to get their work finished.

5. We all can use a good coach. They are able to draw out of us the level of effort we

want to have but do not believe we possess. *"A plan in the heart of a man is like deep water, but a man of understanding draws it out." Proverbs 20:5*
Are you that kind of a coach to others?

6. *"Many a man proclaims his own loyalty but who can find a trustworthy man?" Proverbs 20:6*
Words mean little, it is what we do that counts. *"Well done is better than well said."* - Ben Franklin

7. Children do not realize until they are older how blessed they are to have a father and mother who live their life with integrity. The children have an example to follow. *"A righteous man who walks in his integrity, how blessed are his sons after him." Proverbs 20:7*

8. Those in leadership have the opportunity to eliminate injustice. It comes with the position. Are you using your position to eliminate or foster injustice?

9. We all try to justify ourselves by saying we are not too bad or by comparing ourselves to those who are worse than us. This usually happens when our conscious kicks in or when we get caught doing something we know is wrong. *"Who can*

say "I have cleansed my heart, I am pure of my sin?" Proverbs 20:9

10. God hates fraud. Treat everyone with equal respect when you do business with them.

11. *"A young person distinguishes himself by the work he does; if his conduct is pure and right." Proverbs 20:11*
    If you want to be recognized no matter your age, your work ethic creates that respect.

12. Humility is another character trait of those who are Walking in Wisdom. We must realize that the natural talents we have are gifts from God. *"The hearing ear and the seeing eye, the Lord has made both of them." Proverbs 20:12*

13. There is something about negotiating that makes most people feel good. *"Bad, bad says the buyer; but when he goes his way, then he boasts." Proverbs 20:14*

14. If you have the right information and know how to speak with understanding, it is far better to have this quality than money. Money comes quickly and leaves just as fast. Knowing how to speak well lets you to earn money over and over again.

15. If you co-sign a loan for someone, make sure you receive some kind of collateral for the risk you take. If the person you co-sign for defaults and does not pay the loan, you will have to pay it, but at least you have something for your trouble.

16. Whatever you earn by defrauding someone may feel good at first but in the end is of no use. *"Bread obtained by falsehood is sweet to a man, but afterward his mouth is filled with gravel."* Proverbs 20:17

17. *"Prepare plans by consultation, and make war by wise guidance."* Proverbs 20:18
People spend more time planning and seeking counsel on their vacation than they do on important decisions in their life, like the friends they keep, the work they do, or even who they marry.

18. If you know someone who talks behind a person's back or shares the secrets of others, avoid them because they will do the same to you and with your secrets.

19. Revenge is a feeling we must restrain. Let the Lord repay the evil done to you. How often in sports is the person who retaliates after they were attacked first is the one who ends up with the penalty?

20. ***"Man's steps are ordained by the Lord, how then can man understand his ways?" Proverbs 20:24***
Life must be lived by faith. It is difficult to explain why good things happen to bad people and bad things happen to good people.

21. It is foolish for you to make a commitment to do something and then afterward investigate whether you should have made the commitment.

22. Our spirit is what God uses to convict us of right and wrong. Everyone has a conscious. It is our choice as to whether or not we want to yield to it.

23. Most people will remain in their place of leadership by being loyal, truthful, and doing what is right.

24. We idolized young adults for their strength, their looks, and their youth. It is when they turn older that they become distinguished, provided that wisdom comes with age.

25. There are times when we are injured or physically punished because of doing something wrong. It "leaves a mark" on us so much that it corrects our behavior from doing that wrong again.

Day Twenty-One
Conduct – Part I

1. Those with authority over us have it because this is God's plan right now. We must accept that by faith. Their heart and, thus, the decisions they make is like paths of water in the hand of the Lord. God turns it however He wishes. This means prayer can change things because God is in control.

2. The entire history of man is built on self-justification - thinking that what we do is right in our own eyes. God weighs motives and intentions. I have my opinions, but only God can see into the true motives of my heart.

3. Those who follow religious creeds think that it is more important for them to follow their rules above all else, even if it hurts others. They miss out on the true meaning of their faith, which is to do what is right, to be just and fair.

4. *"The plans of the diligent lead surely to advantage;"* it is one thing to have a plan, it is another to be doing something to make that plan come about. *"But everyone who is hasty comes surely to poverty." Proverbs 21:5*

If you are anxious for results and push something to happen before its time, you will end up worse off than when you started.

5. Fraud that brings you money will fade away. It is really the pursuit of your own death because you may one day defraud the wrong person and end up dead because of it.

6. Another test of one who is Walking in Wisdom is to see how they conduct themselves with their decisions. If they waffle on what is right and wrong, then avoid them. If they are dependable doing what is right, then associate with them.

7. Too many times we think that having it all is what is best. It is better to have little with peace than to have strife and conflict with much.

8. Jesus said that the poor will always be with us. God provides a way for us to help them if we are willing. If we heed their need for help, in turn, when we need help and ask for it, others will help us, too.

9. More times than not, giving some kind of a gift will cause a person's anger to subside and look more favorably on you. Why do you think many a man brings his sweetheart flowers when she is upset?

10. When justice is executed properly and quickly, those who are law abiding rejoice. Those who are wicked live in fear because they know that when caught, they will receive quick retribution for their deeds.

11. Those who walk with wisdom and understanding keep themselves protected because they seek to know more and to do what is right. If they wander and stray from this pursuit, it leads to trouble.

12. *"He who loves pleasure will become a poor man; he who loves wine and oil will not become rich." Proverbs 21:17* Why? It is because they spend their energy and money on what pleases them today and do not understand the principle of delayed gratification.

13. *"The wise man plans for and saves for his future but the foolish person squanders what he has." Proverbs 21:20*

14. *"He who pursues righteousness and loyalty finds life, righteousness and honor." Proverbs 21:21* You reap what you sow and then some because others will respect you for your loyalty and doing what is right.

15. Being wise is better than being strong because if you can figure out how to win

the fight before it begins, you can overcome the stronger person.

16. *"He who guards his mouth and his tongue, guards his soul from trouble." Proverbs 21:23*
Many of the problems we have in our relationships are because of what we say and how we say it.

17. *"He who acts with insolent pride is someone who is proud, haughty, and a scoffer." Proverbs 21:24*

18. Someone who is lazy craves to have what others have, yet they are unwilling to do the work to have it.

19. Do you really think that God cares if you come to Him every day with your prayer or some personal "sacrifice" when the desire of your heart is really about what pleases you?

20. A person who is doing something wrong may come across with boldness in order to cover his evil intentions. This boldness is a smokescreen. Those who are doing what is right are confident and not boastful.

21. *"There is no wisdom and no understanding and no counsel against the Lord." Proverbs 21:30*

22. *"The horse is prepared for the day of battle, but the victory belongs to the Lord." Proverbs 21:31*
I must do my part to prepare ahead of time for any endeavor. I must also realize that the outcome is at God's discretion.

Day Twenty-Two
Conduct – Part II

1. *"A good name is to be more desired than great riches, favor is better than silver and gold." Proverbs 22:1*
   Your character + your reputation = your name. When people hear your name, they have an opinion of you. The better your "name" is, the more doors it will open, the more trust you receive, the more opportunities presented to you. That is why a good name is to be more desired than great riches because money can go as fast as it comes. A good name helps you rebuild your fortune; a bad name limits your options.

2. No matter where you are in life, rich or poor, God created us. Therefore, we have to account to God for our actions.

3. *"The prudent sees the evil and hides himself, but the naïve go on, and are punished for it." Proverbs 22:3*
   Those who are sensible, practical, farsighted, careful, even cautious, look ahead. They study the future and look down the path to see what can cause a problem and avoid it. Those who are reckless, carless, and more interested in what is happening now go forward with

their foolish behavior and suffer the consequences. They have not learned the value of delayed gratification.

4. *"Train up a child in the way he should go, even when he is old he will not depart from it." Proverbs 22:6*
Are you a victim of someone trying to change you from who you are into someone you are not? A classic example is someone who is interested, even gifted, in the arts and does not have much of an interest in competitive athletics. If they are pushed into playing a sport they are not interested in, they end up miserable. Their parents are miserable, too, because the child is out of his or her true element. Look at the personality of your child. Understand your child's interests. It is important to invest time so your child can try many areas so they can discover what their gifts and talents are. Your role as a parent, guardian, or coach is to help them develop their gifts for their enjoyment, not yours.

5. If you borrow money from someone, you are in debt to them. At any time they can come to collect what you owe them, no matter how inconvenient it is for you to repay them. In business, this is having your "note called," meaning you have to pay back what you owe immediately. If

you cannot refinance the loan or come up with the cash, you lose your business. *"The borrower becomes the lender's slave." Proverbs 22:7*

6. *"Drive out the scoffer and contention will go out, even strife and dishonor will cease." Proverbs 22:10*
Want to fix a fragmented team? Root out and get rid of those who are argumentative, those who mock others, and those who show contempt for their fellow workers. If you do not do this, your best team members will leave. We spend a lot of our waking hours working. If we are in an environment that is caustic, we will leave to find a better work environment. Rotten apples spoil the whole barrel. Once you get rid of the "rotten apples," the rest of the apples will be just fine.

7. Leaders are always looking to promote people they can trust and who know how to speak well, meaning they are gracious in how they talk to others. Are you that kind of person?

8. Someone who is lazy will find any reason not to work, no matter how absurd. Our excuses reflect our character.

9. *"Do not rob the poor because he is poor or crush the afflicted because the Lord will come after those who do and the end may be their death."* Proverbs 22:22

10. Avoid a person who always gets angry quickly. If you associate with them long enough, you may become like them and find yourself in trouble because of it. *"Do not associate with a man given to anger; or go with a hot tempered man, lest you learn from his ways, and find a snare for yourself."* Proverbs 22:24

11. Avoid, if at all possible, being responsible for someone else's debt. If they do not pay then you are responsible to pay for them. And if you do not have the money, you are going to lose what you have to pay off their debt.

12. *"Do you see a man skilled in his work? He will stand before kings; he will not stand before obscure men."* Proverbs 22:29

Day Twenty Three
Evaluation

1. It is important to be wise when you eat with someone in leadership or authority. Watching how a person eats, what their table manners are like, is a good way to judge their character. Is the person considerate of others? Does the person take an extra-large portion of food for themselves? Did they outreach someone else for the food? How do they treat the staff serving the meal? Is their main focus on getting their food and eating? These are indicators to see if the person has or lacks self-control. In other words, does his appetite control him? The person may not be dependable because their indulgences can influence their decisions.

2. It is important to have the right perspective on gaining wealth. Work hard, and then save what earn. You cross the line when becoming wealthy consumes you so much that this obsession becomes your god. Money comes and goes. If you consume yourself with chasing wealth you will find that you can never have enough. Your obsession creates misery for those around you and for yourself.

3. ***"As a man thinks within himself, so he is." Proverbs 23:7***
   There has been much written about this passage. It is one of the base beliefs that, based on how you think, will determine the outcome of who you are. I believe in the power of optimism. There is plenty of evidence using the placebo testing that people can feel better just by believing the pill they took has the power to heal them. The context of this passage is a warning not to eat with a selfish man or desire his treats (what he indulges). The selfish man encourages you to eat and drink with him but it is insincere. He does not want to share what he has with you. If you find that you are insincere in your gift giving, you too may be a selfish man.

4. Those who teach or coach, as well as parents, feel a sense of pride when their children are wise in their decisions. ***"...if your heart is wise, my own heart also will be glad." Proverbs 23:15***

5. Every generation must fight the good fight of faith and stand for what is right. All of us fall victim to envy. We envy those who sin and seem to get away with it because we wonder why we cannot do the same. We need to live in reverence to God and His sense of right and wrong. We are instructed to be wise and direct our heart

in the right way. We receive instruction to be careful with who we associate with. Those who over indulge in satisfying their desires end in poverty and loss. *"Do not let your heart envy sinners, but live in the fear of the Lord always." Proverbs 23:17*

6. As a parent, my desire was to raise both good children and wise adults. Children, it is up to you to decide how you will live your life. Will you strive for wisdom, get understanding, and instruction? *Proverbs 23:22-23*

7. One of the keys to wisdom is listening. The temptation to be unfaithful to your spouse is all around us. Add easy access to internet pornography, and it seems the odds are against you. Will you be one of the faithful? *Proverbs 23:26-28*

8. Drinking alcohol is customary in most cultures. Alcohol changes the chemical makeup in the body. There are those who drink too much and then complain the next day of the hangover they have or how sick they feel. Some drink so much they do not remember what they did or what harm they caused. Drunk driving kills; yet, when the night is over, when the hangover ends, the habit to drink in excess remains. The cycle starts again.

Do you drink? Do you drink in excess?
Do you care?   *Proverbs 23:29-33*

Day Twenty-Four
The People You Meet

1. There are those who do evil and do not suffer the consequences of their actions. It is tempting for us to envy them. However, avoid these people because of the way they think. Their minds look for ways to take advantage of others and not caring who they hurt in the process. If you associate with them, you will become like them. And you will suffer at their hands because they will take advantage of you as well.

2. ***"By wisdom a house is built, and by understanding it is established; and by knowledge the rooms are filled with all precious and pleasant riches."***
Proverbs 24:3
A house is a metaphor for just about anything that you want to be permanent in your life. If you build it with wisdom and understanding, it will stand for a long time. You pick the right foundation on which to build and then use quality materials to build it. Same with furnishing the inside of the house, you use knowledge and fill your rooms appropriately.

3. *"A wise man is strong, and a man of knowledge increases power. For by wise guidance you will wage war, and in the abundance of counselors there is victory." Proverbs 24:5*

   You know the phrase *"knowledge is power."* This may be where it came from. The more you know and the more you use knowledge properly, the more power you can have. Power comes in many different ways. It is important to remember that wisdom is required to take right action. Sometimes it takes more power not to act. Wisdom seeks out counselors, those who can give guidance. If heeded, victory is the result.

4. *"If you fail under pressure, your strength is too small." Proverbs 24:10*

   Times of trouble bring out the true character of a person. If you poke a hole in a bag with liquid inside, whatever is inside will come flowing out. Put a man in a challenging situation, and most men will react according to their character. If they lack self-control, then they will lash out. If they are fearful, they will shrink back. How do you react during times of trouble? Do you remain even in your temperament, or do you have emotional swings? Leaders need to remain calm; this does not mean you are not afraid, or worried, or concerned. It means you demonstrate to others that you can be relied on when the "going gets tough." Dr. Martin Luther King, Jr. says it well *"The ultimate measure of a man is not where he stands in moments of comfort and convenience, but where he stands at times of challenge and controversy..."*

5. Everyone wants justice and fairness in the way they are treated. Some take advantage of others because of the color of their skin, the way they look, the language they speak, the money they do not have, or their gender. If we see this happening, it is our responsibility to help them so they are not taken advantage of. Also, it is important to be honest with yourself. If you do not help but had the chance to, fess up to it. Hiding behind some lame excuse that you "did not know what was going on," only makes you dishonest. God knows. We cannot hide.

6. Wisdom, like honey to the tongue, is sweet for your soul. If you understand that, you will always find the right way to go.

7. How many times do we feel good when something bad happens to someone we consider to be our "enemy"? It is easy to do this but God may not see it the same

way. Jesus tells us to pray for our enemies (and that does not mean to pray that bad things happen to them). It means to pray for their betterment.

8. Another battle we have is feeling anxious and worrisome because of the evil people do. We may feel envious of those who are defrauding others and getting away with their actions, while we struggle financially or relationally by doing what is right. Their time will come. If not in this life, it will in the next. Remain faithful to what is good and right. Do not be named with those who do evil.

9. This is a wise saying: *"to show partiality in judgment is not good." Proverbs 24:23* We all want fairness and justice. So when someone treats those who do wrong as though they did what is right, others curse them. Also, when someone stands up for what is right and calls evil for what it is, people bless them and praise them.

10. Many times we rush to do something before preparing for the future. One of those things is marriage. It is important to secure how you will earn your wages first, and then look to start a family. *"Prepare your work outside, and make it ready for yourself in the field; afterwards, then, build your house." Proverbs 24:27*

11. Be honest and do not lie to get someone in trouble, especially if they tried to do the same to you. Have you ever watched a football game when someone takes a cheap shot at another player and the one who strikes back is the one who gets "caught" by the referees? Same thing here; just because you can, does not mean you should.

12. Laziness leads to poverty. Poverty can mean more than lacking money. You can be poor in character, poor in discipline, or poor in affections. If you neglect what is right on purpose, because you are lazy or do not think it is important, you will find those areas of your life getting worse. You may not recognize it because you are in the midst of it. You do not "see the forest from the trees," but others do. *"A little sleep, a little slumber, a little folding of the hands to rest. Then your poverty will come as a robber, and your want like an armed man." Proverbs 24:33-34*

Day Twenty-Five
Relationships – Part I

1. We all want to know what others are thinking. The heavens are immeasurable and so are the true thoughts of others.

2. The purification of metals through heating produces dross, or what is worthless, so you can get to the pure silver or gold. The metal then becomes something a craftsman can work with. The same is true for your organization or business. If you remove those who are malicious, cutting, and disrespectful, your company will be established and known for doing what is right.

3. How many times have you walked into a banquet room and wondered where you should sit? It is best to be modest and sit in an inconspicuous place and have the one who is throwing the event ask you to sit closer or with them. This benefits you in two ways. The first is for the positive. Everyone at the event will see you moving to the head table. Second, this saves you from embarrassment. What if you sit in a spot that is reserved for someone else and then are asked to move to a different table?

4. If you have something against another person, first gather all your evidence. Keep the matter private until you are ready with all the facts. This benefits your case because the one you want to approach will not find out what you are doing, and you can gather your facts unnoticed. If you make the matter publically known before gathering your facts your reputation may suffer because others may call you a gossip and spreading false rumors.

5. Jewelry, put into the right setting, is a work of art; it is beautiful and makes you feel wonderful. The same feeling comes when someone speaks the right words to you at the right time to build you up or helps you. It may be a word of correction, yet it has the same effect because they do it in such a way that you can receive it as instruction. ***"Like apples of gold in settings of silver is a word spoken in right circumstances." Proverbs 25:11***

6. Be careful what you say. Avoid being boastful or a braggart. Someone who exaggerates what they say creates disappointment and distrust.

7. Self-control is a component of the Fruit of the Spirit. If you find something you enjoy, enjoy it. Yet enjoy it in moderation

and not in excess. One dessert is tasty; two is too much; three, and you lack control.

8. There is a saying: *"good fences make for good neighbors."* The wisdom behind this saying is to visit your neighbors rarely and not to overstay your time with them. If not, they will come to despise your visits and look to avoid you.

9. If someone tells lies about someone else, chances are they tell lies about you. A person who does this hurts and harms with their words. Words can hurt, not just sticks and stones.

10. Trust is something to be treasured. Being able to trust someone with a task or a job is priceless. It is similar when you trust your teeth when you eat something. You bite down, start chewing, and all of a sudden your tooth cracks. The pain you feel is excruciating. Trusting someone with a task or a job that they do not do hurts.

11. Imagine you are outside for an event, and it is colder than you expected. You want a jacket, a blanket, or something to keep you warm. How do you feel when someone notices and takes their jacket off and gives it to you to wear? You feel both

grateful and warm. The same is true when someone is hurting and you encourage them with kind words that lift their spirit. *"Like one who takes off a garment on a cold day, or like vinegar on soda, is he who sings songs to a troubled heart." Proverbs 25:20*

12. Alexander the Great, after defeating Darius, took captive his wife and mother. Instead of treating them as his enemy, he treated them with the royalty they were accustomed to. This demonstration of kindness increased his reputation and embarrassed Darius. *"If your enemy is hungry, give him food to eat; and if he is thirsty, give him water to drink; for you will heap burning coals on his head, and the Lord will reward you." Proverbs 25:21-22*

13. There are certain signals in the sky that when we see them we can predict the weather like dark billowing clouds, thunder and lightning. The same is true with someone with a vicious tongue. Someone who speaks with cutting, biting words stirs up anger in others.

14. Abundance of strife is a life no one wants. It is better to have and share a small house with someone who is kind than a large mansion with a contentious person;

someone who looks to argue, is antagonistic, combative and touchy.

15. We all like good news. Especially when we hear from those who live far away from us. It is like taking a cold drink on a hot day. It feels good.

16. Remember the last time you worked outside on a hot day? You feel thirsty and dehydrated. So you go and get a drink of water expecting it to be cool and clean. Yet the water is dirty and it smells. How do you feel? Betrayed? Let down? Disappointed? The same feeling occurs when someone you look up to and believe lives a life of trustworthiness - someone who stood up for what is right and just gives way to what is evil and wrong. *"Like a trampled spring and a polluted well is a righteous man who gives way before the wicked." Proverbs 25:26*

17. Excess, in any form, is not good; nor is it good for a person to seek recognition and fame. Recognition and fame feeds the vanity in our soul and is never satisfied.

18. Self-control is a defense mechanism against our impulses and desires. Imagine a castle with no walls. It has no way to protect itself from its enemies. The same is true for the man who lacks self-

control. When his desires kick in, he is at the mercy of those desires. *"Like a city that is broken into and without walls is a man who has no control over his spirit." Proverbs 25:28*

Day Twenty-Six
Relationships – Part II

1. We all know when something is just not right. Imagine you are a farmer and you want to harvest your crop. Instead of it being sunny, it is raining. This does not make for pleasant work. The same is true when you see someone who is acting like a fool and receiving fame and recognition. A prime example is the entertainment industry.

2. If you want to turn a horse or a donkey, you put a bridle in their mouth to move them in the direction you want them to go. When dealing with someone that is acting like a fool, one way to correct their behavior is to get their attention; one way may be by embarrassing them.

3. If you find yourself around someone acting and talking like a fool (someone whose behavior lacks wisdom), it is best to respond to them in a way their foolish behavior deserves rather than tolerate their actions. This reminds them and serves as a warning to others watching that this behavior is not tolerated.

4. Listening to a fool give advice makes as much sense as trying to walk when you

are unable to stand. It creates frustration and pain.

5. Hiring the right people is critical to a business' success. If you refuse to pay attention to your hiring practices, you will hire anyone who seems to fit and soon realize they do not. Adopt a proven method that screens the applicants to find out their work ethic and behavior in given situations. How they acted in the past is a good indication on how they will act when employed by you.

6. Arrogance clouds good judgment. *"There is more hope for someone acting like a fool to change than someone who is wise in their own eyes." Proverbs 26:12*

7. Someone who is lazy will always find an excuse not to do something; even if it sounds absurd to you, it will not to them. *"There is a lion in the road! A lion is in the open square." Proverbs 26:13*

8. Disagreeing with someone who is lazy is worse than disagreeing with people who have a different point of view than you do. It is tough to convince a lazy person that they are wrong because they have no interest in being right, which means they have no interest in learning. Those who differ from your point of view are open to

correction because they want to be accurate and are willing to admit when they are wrong.

9. It is unwise to go up to a dog and grab it by the ears. Chances are the dog will react to attack you. The same is true when you involve yourself with someone else's argument that you have no idea to what is going on. You become the one they turn their anger to. Now this does not mean you turn your back if someone is being hurt or injured. The risk to help someone in need outweighs self-preservation. It is about understanding the situation and not jumping into arguments that you have no cause to be involved with.

10. How do you feel when you find someone who is thoughtless in their actions, reckless in their behavior towards you, and it causes you problems? Then they say to you, "Can't you take a joke? I was just kidding."

11. If you do not add wood to a fire, it will eventually go out. Tend a fire and it will burn a long time. If you tolerate people who gossip or tells lies or allow those who quarrel and create strife to remain in your business, you will have problems. If you

remove them, the problems they cause go away.

12. Be aware that if you tolerate people who gossip, what they say can influence those who listen to them. If it is something that damages your reputation or the reputation of your company, it can be difficult to change people's impressions and perceptions.

13. Discernment is crucial to success in everything you do. You must determine when someone is disguising their evil intent with kind words or through an appearance of kindness towards you.

14. One way to determine if someone is truthful in their words and actions is to find out their reputation from others. Seek references who know the person to determine if they can be trusted. This is not foolproof but it is helpful. We know of stories of individuals who received a good reference and turned out to be a swindler. One consideration to help you is the old saying, "If it seems too good to be true, it probably is." Also, check your motives. What is driving you to take action? Are you feeling greedy? Are you feeling down, that you deserve more? We are far more tempted when those feelings are

upon us and we are vulnerable to make poor choices.

Day Twenty-Seven
The Actions We Take – Part I

1. You have heard the phrase, *"Don't count your chickens before they are hatched."* A different way of saying this is, ***"Do not boast about tomorrow for you do not know what a day may bring forth."***
   Proverbs 27:1
   Whatever we expect to happen may not happen. Boasting demonstrates arrogance. If something does not happen the way you "boasted" it will, it brings discouragement and embarrassment. Walking in Wisdom means expecting a good outcome but not bragging about it before it happens.

2. It is best if we let other praise us and give us good publicity than for us to tell others about how good we are.

3. The weight one feels when lifting a heavy stone or a bag of sand is lighter than the feeing one feels when being provoked to anger by a fool.

4. Jealousy is an overwhelming feeling and those who succumb to it are unpredictable with their behavior.

5. *"Open rebuke is better than love concealed." Proverbs 27:5*
   Love requires expression or it is not real love.

6. *"Faithful are the wounds of a friend, but deceitful are the kisses of an enemy." Proverbs 27:6*
   A loyal friend may hurt you through correction, but those are wounds that help and heal. An enemy will give you sweet compliments that offer no real value.

7. Sometimes, the more possessions a person has, the less they value what they have. Yet to those who have little to nothing, the most inexpensive things seem valuable. Those who do not lack food seem to be the pickiest of eaters; those who are hungry have little problem eating what some would consider distasteful.

8. Birds build their nests away from danger in secure and safe places. When the bird wanders far from their nest, they endanger themselves. The same goes for a man who wanders from his home in search of pleasure. The further a man goes from his home, the temptation towards infidelity increases. When temptation has its way, sin follows. Maybe that is why many people like the

Las Vegas branding, *"What happens in Vegas, stays in Vegas."*

9. We all enjoy the sweet smell of certain fragrances and perfumes. It makes us feel good. The same is true when you receive good advice or guidance from a friend. It makes you feel good, too.

10. It is best to cultivate friends that are close by because you never know when you will need their help. Having family members far away who can help is not as good as having a friend close by when you are in need.

11. How you conduct yourself is a reflection on your parents, your teachers, your coach, and your manager, as well as yourself. As you walk in wisdom it proves that they were right in their instructions.

12. ***"A prudent man sees evil and hides himself, they naïve proceed and pay the penalty." Proverbs 27:12***
One who is cautious, alert, pragmatic, careful and sensible about what is going on around him sees down the road as to what is happening and then avoids it. The one who is gullible, immature, and foolish does not pay attention to what is going on and proceeds with his actions and pays the penalty for his behavior. The

circumstances we find ourselves in is, for the most part, a direct result of the choices we make.

13. It is better not to make a loud boastful compliment of a friend before they do the work you asked them to do because if they do not do it, it feels more like a curse than a blessing.

14. *"A contestant dripping on a day of steady rain and a contentious woman are alike; he would restrain her restrains the wind, and grasps oil with his right hand." Proverbs 27:15*
Someone whose personality is combative, argumentative, quarrelsome, and touchy is hard to change, just like it is hard to grasp oil in your hand.

15. One way to become better is through competition; having an antagonist. We do not like when we are up against an opponent but the opponent forces us to work harder and think better. *"Iron sharpens iron, so one man sharpens another." Proverbs 27:17*

16. Jesus said that *"out of the heart, a man speaks." Matthew 12:34*
He meant that we cannot hide what is in our heart. When we talk, our true character comes out in what we say.

When we look into a mirror we see our physical self. What we say reflects what is in our heart.

17. God created man with an inner desire to do more, have more, *"Be fruitful and multiply, and fill the earth, and subdue it; and rule over the fish of the sea and over the birds of the sky, and over every living thing that moves on the earth" Genesis 1:28*
Ever since man's first sin in the Garden of Eden, he looks for satisfaction away from God and what God created for him. Until one returns to God, satisfaction and contentment is not found. Just like death is never satisfied, the natural man without God is never satisfied.

18. Praise given to us is a test of our character because it reveals how we handle the praise. Just like heat brings out the real quality of gold, so a man, when given praise, demonstrates true humility or excessive pride.

19. I said before that there is a large difference with a person who has ten years of true work experience and a person who has one year of experience that they repeat for ten years. One truly is growing; the other is stagnant. You must take responsibility for your income. It

does not matter if you work for someone else or own your own business. In either case, you are your own "business owner." Anything can happen to your job or business, and you need to take care of how you build your career. It is up to you; if you leave it to someone else, you will be disappointed.

Day Twenty-Eight
The Actions We Take - Part II

1. The king of the beasts is the lion. Some say lions never retreat. The righteous are as confident as a lion but the wicked run when no one is pursuing them. Confidence (not arrogance) comes from doing right.

2. A person can have great influence over a nation who possesses understanding and knowledge and does what is right; they can set a nation on the right path.

3. The devastation a hard rain has when it creates a flood that leaves no vegetation is like those who take from the poor and keeps them poor.

4. Your conviction in doing what is right will determine your tolerance of those who do wrong.

5. *"Better is the poor who walks in his integrity, than he who is crooked though he be rich." Proverbs 28:6*
   Doing right is better than being rich if it means compromising your integrity.

6. If you are reckless with your money, you create a bad name for those who raised

you to be better than that. You lack of self-control.

7. If you take advantage of the poor for your financial gain you are actually creating a savings account for someone who is gracious to the poor.

8. Do not be deceived. God does not respect the prayer of someone who defies doing what is right and just.

9. Those who attempt to lead people who are upright in their behavior into doing evil will only lead himself into his own trap of doom.

10. People rejoice when those who do right win.

11. ***"He who conceals his transgressions will not prosper, but he who confesses and forsakes them will find compassion." Proverbs 28:13***
How many times have we seen transgressions from our elected officials or those who are in high profile positions? Some deny it, and we see the media becomes even more interested in uncovering the real story. Others "come clean," admit they did wrong, say they are sorry, are quickly forgiven, and some even keep their position.

12. Blessing is on the one who guards against sin and its consequences by listening to their conscience; those who harden their heart and do not listen fall into calamity.

13. Leadership is no longer "command and control," those who lead like this lack understanding and will not last long in their role.

14. In business, it is important to focus; pick your priorities. Too many times, one pursues many options and they may lead to dead ends and possibly even bankruptcy.

15. Steady pursuit of a goal is better than being hasty to cut corners to try to reach the goal faster.

16. Some men, for the smallest of bribes, will depart from what is right. Be careful if you come across such a person because they cannot be trusted. *"To show partiality is not good because for a piece of bread a man will transgress." Proverbs 28:21*

17. Honesty in your dealings with someone is the best course of action to take because even if you correct them, they will have more respect for you than if you flattered them and did not call them out on their problem.

18. There are plenty of people who take advantage of their parents' generosity just because they are their parents. They rob their parents but are telling others that their parents are good people helping them out. If a person does this and you know about it, avoid them because they will look to take advantage of you, too, just as they are ok with destroying their parents by taking money from them.

19. *"He who gives to the poor will never want, but he who shuts his eyes will have many curses." Proverbs 28:27*
This is about self-deception. The poor are all around, and there are many ways one can help.

Day Twenty-Nine
The Actions We Take – Part III

1. Refusing correction over and over again makes you numb to it and leads to disaster. The path you chose by not listening to those who try to give you guidance leads to problems.

2. Everyone knows when a righteous person is at the helm of an organization or a country. The people rejoice when this happens. The same is true when someone leading them is immoral and depraved. People cry out in pain and grief.

3. As a parent, we feel good when our children walk in wisdom. We know that if our children give into their lusts and lack self-control, it can lead them to financial ruin as well as moral corruption.

4. It is hard work to lead an organization properly, doing what is right, just, and fair as the basis for advancement. It is even harder when someone you rely on to support you plays favorites and accept gifts for advancement. This will overthrow all of your efforts.

5. If you flatter your neighbor and are not sincere in your compliments you run the risk of helping them stay blinded to their shortcomings. *"A man who flatters his neighbor, is spreading a net for his steps." Proverbs 29:5*

6. *"By transgression an evil man is ensnared, but the righteous sings and rejoices." Proverbs 29:6*
If you chose to do wrong, you trap yourself into doing wrong. The more you do something, the more it becomes a habit and it is harder to break free. Those who avoid this behavior never have this problem.

7. There are two kinds of people: those who concern themselves with the poor and look to do something about it, and those who do not even comprehend that there is a problem.

8. Those who mock, belittle, and ridicule are the ones who stir up discord; they create feelings and unbalanced emotions in people. Those who are wise and act in wisdom are the ones who keep people calm.

9. One definition of a fool is someone who is so set on their point of view that they argue with you even though they are

wrong. They may get angry with you or laugh at you. Either way, it is not a pleasant conversation.

10. The more someone hates another person, the easier it is to justify hurting them - even killing them, regardless if they are blameless and did no wrong. This hatred blinds them to find reasons to justify their actions. Those who are upright in their character look to help those who suffer at the hands of this hatred.

11. Another test to find out if someone is a fool is to see if they keep or lose their temper often. A fool must be right and will argue immediately to support their point of view. A wise man will hold back to find out as much as possible before answering.

12. How a leader deals with lies and gossip will determine the kind of people who work for them. The more the leader allows lying and gossip to happen, the more their subordinates will act as if lying and gossip is acceptable behavior and then practice it themselves. Chances are they will go even further in their behavior to do harm to others.

13. Children require boundaries for their behavior so they can know right from

wrong. If they do something wrong, correction is required. If they do something right, praise is required. Both actions give the child guidance. Without proper correction, a child will not understand proper boundaries and will cross over them to their harm, to others harm, and your shame.

14. When those who act wickedly increase, then it is safe to say that crime increases also.

15. If a parent who corrects his or her child during their formative years, the child will, most likely repay the parent with delight in their behavior as an adult.

16. If a family, company, or even a country does not have a vision, a goal, or mission, they end up going in all sorts of directions. There is no common purpose to rally around. A vision or a mission is the common purpose that keeps people focused each and every day. Like an army platoon, they know exactly what they and their fellow soldiers are doing on the mission; if they do not, someone dies. When there is a mission and everyone knows their role to accomplish the mission, everyone is more engaged and feels responsible for their assignments.

"Where there is no vision, the people perish." Proverbs 29:18

17. *"A servant will not be instructed by words alone, for though he understands, there will be no response."* Proverbs 29:19
    This verse goes to the core of the human condition. If someone works for you and is willfully unresponsive to correct their behavior, additional measures are needed. The worker may know there is a problem. One course of action I use is a formal Performance Improvement Plan (PIP). It is used to identify the problem(s) with an agreed upon set of tasks that need to be performed. All within a certain time frame. The subordinate agrees to the PIP and if their behavior changes, all good. If their behavior does not match the agreed upon PIP, the agreement is dismissal. They, not you, are responsible for the dismissal. You are just carrying out the agreement. This process demonstrates to all that there are consequences to one's behavior.

18. Be on the lookout when someone is hasty or impulsive with their words. Their willingness to commit to something before they really understand what they are agreeing to can lead to problems. Any connection you have to that person may

cause you to suffer because of their impulsiveness.

19. Those who have an angry temperament stir up discord, fighting, friction, and conflict. They create an atmosphere of misbehavior if unchecked.

20. *"A man's pride will bring him low, but a humble spirit will obtain honor."* *Proverbs 29:23*
    When I read this, it reminds me so much of professional athletes. The one who comes to mind for me with a humble spirit is Cal Ripken, Jr. Who do you know that exemplifies a humble spirit? Who do you know that their pride brought them low?

21. Who you partner with tells much about yourself. If you partner with a thief and know it going in, you demonstrate a disrespect for yourself. It shows that you are willing to go to jail or lose all you have to be associated with one who willingly defrauds people.

22. *"The fear of man brings a snare, but he who trusts in the Lord will be exalted."* *Proverbs 29:25*
    Trust in God's plan for your life. We stumble when we look to others to help us to accomplish what we want to

accomplish. We become hasty, foolish, and impulsive so we can have "it" now.

23. We tend to look to those in authority for justice. True justice comes from the Lord.

24. Those who do what is right are offensive and repulsive to those who do wrong; and vice versa.

Day Thirty
Words to Live By

1. The one who is wise realizes how little they know. They recognize how devoid of knowledge they really have when they compare themselves with God and His infinite wisdom.

2. God gave us a guidebook of principles to live our lives with. Every word provided is there to help guide and protect us. If we add our own rules based on opinion, we water down its essence. If we take words away from what He says, we compromise its value.

3. Our instructor from Proverbs asks for two things in his life; one is to keep deception and lies far from him and the other is to give him neither poverty nor riches. He wants only what is enough because if he has too much, he knows himself well enough that he will think he is the cause of his riches and forget to give God the glory. If he has too little, he knows himself that he will look to steal, and because of this behavior, profane God's reputation with his sin.

4. Arrogance is demonstrated by actions and attitudes. Those who are arrogant lack

gratefulness, especially to their parents. They think they are wholesome when they are not. And they look down on others as being less important than they are.

5. There are people who speak with such biting words that when you hear them, they feel like they are stabbing you with a knife. They do not seem to care who they hurt, especially those in need.

6. *"The leech has two daughters, "Give", "Give." Proverbs 30:15*
A leech attaches itself to an animal and lives off of their blood. It must be removed and it will not leave on its own. Be careful of those who see to be asking you to give them something. Out of kindness you will. Yet they will not stop asking on their own and thus take advantage of your kindness.

7. Solomon shares with us that there are things in life which consumes what it's given: a fire and the grave.

8. Solomon, who is the wisest of men, also shares with us that there are things which he did not understand and needs further explanation because of their complexity, like a man and a woman in love.

9. Those who are habitually unfaithful are callous from their behavior. They do what

they do and then justify it by saying they did nothing wrong.

10. There are four results which make it hard to be around people because of their arrogance: when someone all of a sudden goes from poor to rich or no authority to great authority because the power makes them think they can get away with anything; a fool who does not know how to control himself after over indulging with eating and drinking; a woman who finally finds a husband and is boastful because of it; and someone who before was hired help and is now running the operation.

11. Wisdom comes in small packages. Ants prepare for hard times because you see them storing away food in the summer. The rock badgers use the rocks for their protection against predators. The locusts all move about as one army even though there is no leader. The little geckos or lizards that you can pick up in your hand show up in the most expensive homes.

12. There are four things which are quite confident in their movement: the lion, the strutting rooster, the male ram, and a leader who has his army with him.

13. You still have time to change the road you are on. If you do not, the consequences

of your actions will come your way. *"For the churning of milk produces butter, and the pressing of the nose brings forth blood; so the churning of anger produces strife." Proverbs 30:33*

Day Thirty-One
Who You Want to Be

1. As a leader, you set the example. A person must evaluate how he lives his life. Are you using your time or wasting it? People are controlled by their lusts. Lusts for physical pleasure as well as emotional pleasures. Some turn to eating, sex, or drinking. Drinking alcohol to the point of forgetting what you did, said, or promised, creates problems for you and those you made promises to.

2. We must open our mouths and defend or protect the unfortunate, especially those who are unable to speak for themselves. We must defend the rights of the afflicted and those in need.

3. This section talks about a man finding an exceptional wife; the principles are the same if you want to be an exceptional husband, too.

    a. An excellent wife is a much better find than having expensive jewelry because both money and jewelry can be replaced. Quality of character, trust, and loyalty are much harder to find.

b. Trust is the next area of importance; when there is trust, there is no lack of gain in the relationship.

c. Both look to do good for the other person each and every day.

d. They are creative, looking to make things better.

e. They are like merchants, seeking the good things that have true value and are not just for show.

f. They sacrifice their own sleep for the betterment of the family and demonstrate appreciation to those who help the family.

g. They are good with their finances. They look for ways to improve their income and savings by investing in what produces positive cash flow.

h. They are health conscious. They look for ways to be and stay healthy.

i. There is no task that is too petty, small, or menial. If something needs doing, they do it.

j. They demonstrate kindness and generosity to those in need and to the poor.

k. The future holds no fear to them because they prepare for rainy days and financial hard times.

l. There is a sense of modesty in how they dress. They do not dress to impress others, but rather dress appropriately.

m. They look for ways to increase their income by either making things or buying and reselling them.

n. A strong character and self-respect is what they favor; not the clothes they wear, the house they live in, or the car they drive.

o. They are students of wisdom; they love to teach others how to be wise.

p. There is no attitude of laziness or hiding from work; they look for ways to help out.

q. Their children and their spouse praise them and say good things about them when they are out in public.

> i. *"Many have done nobly, but you excel them all. Charm is deceitful and beauty is vain, but a woman who fears the Lord, she shall be praised."*
> *Proverbs 31:29-30*

r. In the end, the byproduct of their efforts is what they are praised for.

www.ingramcontent.com/pod-product-compliance
Lightning Source LLC
Chambersburg PA
CBHW060156050426
42446CB00013B/2847